5 minutes TO MORE GREAT REAL ESTATE LETTERS

USEFUL NOTES FOR TOP-SELLING AGENTS

JOHN D. MAYFIELD

ABR®, ABRM, GRI, e-PRO®, CRB

CENGAGE
Learning™

Australia • Brazil • Japan • Korea • Mexico • Singapore • Spain • United Kingdom • United States

5 Minutes to More Great Real Estate Letters: Useful Notes for Top-Selling Agents, Second Edition

John D. Mayfield

Vice President/Editorial Director: Dave Shaut

Acquisitions Editor: Sara Glassmeyer

Development Editor: Arlin Kauffman, LEAP Publishing Services

Senior Marketing and Sales Manager: Mark Linton

Production Manager: Jean Buttrom

Senior Manufacturing Buyer: Charlene Taylor

Senior Art Director: Pamela Galbreath

Production House/Compositor: PreMediaGlobal

Content Project Management: PreMediaGlobal

Senior Rights Acquisitions Specialist: John Hill

Cover Designer: Cindy Baldwin

Cover Image: Finding a House © iStockphoto.com/Helder Almeida

Library of Congress Control Number: 2010942695

Student Edition ISBN 13: 978-1-111-42819-8
Student Edition ISBN 10: 1-111-42819-0

Student Edition with CD ISBN 13: 978-1-111-42818-1
Student Edition with CD ISBN 10: 1-111-42818-2

Cengage Learning
5191 Natorp Boulevard
Mason, OH 45040
USA

Cengage Learning is a leading provider of customized learning solutions with office locations around the globe, including Singapore, the United Kingdom, Australia, Mexico, Brazil, and Japan. Locate your local office at: **international.cengage.com/region**

Cengage Learning products are represented in Canada by Nelson Education, Ltd.

For your course and learning solutions, visit **academic.cengage.com**

Purchase any of our products at your local college store or at our preferred online store **www.cengagebrain.com**

Printed in the United States of America
1 2 3 4 5 6 7 15 14 13 12 11

DEDICATION

To my wife, Kerry. She has always been such an inspiration and help to me. I truly would not have the joy and enthusiasm I have for this career in real estate if it were not for her. Thank you Kerry for being such a special and wonderful person in my life, and most of all for being a great wife!

TABLE OF CONTENTS

Foreword vii

Introduction ix

How to Use This Book.. xi

Prospecting...1

Short Sales 59

Sphere of Influence 71

Letters to Buyers..87

Letters to Sellers 127

E-mails and Letters to Other Agents 169

Letters to Vendors 183

Follow-Up Letters 191

PR Letters 199

Referral Letters /E-Mails 207

Letters from Broker 213

Faxes and E-Mails for Scanned Documents.............................231

Conclusion 241

FOREWORD

Communicating quickly and effectively with customers and clients is essential to your business. How you market yourself is essential to your business success! Avid real estate speaker and trainer, John Mayfield, has shown you how to get started with this in his 5-Minute Series books, specifically *5 Minutes to a Great Real Estate Letter*. Once you have the basics, get ready to accelerate the process by using John's new book *5 Minutes to More Great Real Estate Letters*.

John will help you raise the professionalism bar with *5 Minutes to More Great Real Estate Letters*. Now you have more letters to increase your professionalism and set yourself apart with differentiation by blending your strengths and skills using John's advanced tips and tools. Not only do you need an Internet presence, but you also need to reach out to your connections through the use of social media strategies. The suggestions, letters, tips and tools allow you to stand out further as a unique, qualified professional real estate agent, and help you **exceed** the ever-changing real estate needs of today's educated buyers and sellers.

Who doesn't want to go from good to great? Who doesn't want to save time and money? Who doesn't want to stand above the crowd? By combining your acquired skills with these new tools, you are sure to connect with your customers and clients. You are sure to communicate regularly by using the systems and continue to hone your skills to take your business and professionalism to the next level. Albert Einstein said, "Logic will take you from A to B. Imagination will take you everywhere." Imagine where your communication skills could be if you practiced them regularly and challenged yourself to new opportunities. You can customize everything made available to you in John Mayfield's book. By combining your creativity with the tools gained in this book, it will be a win-win situation for all parties involved.

I encourage you to use this book and CD in several ways. First, communicate, communicate, and communicate! Second, choose the correspondence and methods that will work best for you. Finally, work smarter not harder. Don't lose business because you did not communicate quickly enough! Your customers and clients will see how professional you are as you provide the solutions they need. By utilizing the suggestions and tools in this book, your business and professionalism will soar to new heights! With John's help, you can succeed and reach higher than you imagined possible!

The best part is to realize that, with John's help, you are only 5 minutes to your next best real estate letter.

Best regards,
Terry Murphy, RCE, ePRO, GRI
Director of Education
Missouri Association of REALTORS®

INTRODUCTION

Communicating with customers and clients is an important role for the real estate professional and an integral part of the transaction. In order to have a long and prosperous real estate career, agents must understand this necessary element of the sales process. Unfortunately, staying in touch with customers and clients can be difficult with all the daily tasks and responsibilities a real estate professional faces. Sometimes it seems just plain difficult to accomplish.

5 Minutes to More Great Real Estate Letters is designed to help lighten your load and ease the burden of communicating with clients and customers, sphere of influence, and others regularly. In this book you will find a wide variety of prospecting letters, follow-up letters, e-mail messages, fax templates, and more available for you to use.

Yes, this is a letters book, and I encourage you to send letters and e-mail correspondence regularly. However, remind yourself that it's also important to follow up with your customers and clients by phone and in person. People appreciate a personal contact, whether it's through letters, phone calls, or a personal visit. Incorporating this plan of action into your daily routine will help you stay far above and in front of the competition.

I'm excited to make this 2nd edition of *5 Minutes to More Great Real Estate Letters*, and I hope that you find it a valuable resource. I appreciate and thank everyone for all the nice comments about my previous edition of *5 Minutes to a Great Real Estate Letter,* Cengage Learning. That book has been successful and received many wonderful notes and positive feedback. I trust and hope that you will find this book as beneficial as the last one.

Many of the letters in this book are designed as general real estate letters; however, most of the correspondence contained could also be used as e-mail templates. Therefore, I have tried to keep most of the letters concise and to the point. With today's busy lifestyles and many challenges everyone faces daily, it is my belief and experience that shorter, more concise pieces of correspondence work better for most individuals.

I encourage you to take time and watch the video on the enclosed CD-ROM to learn more about how to use the letters, e-mail templates, and other resources. My entire goal is for you to be just *5 Minutes to More Great Real Estate Letters*! I feel certain that with the tools and information in this book and CD-ROM, you are ready to send a professional business correspondence in five minutes or less.

Enjoy the book, and thank you for your business!
John D. Mayfield

Acknowledgments

It was a joy and an honor to hear from my publisher, Cengage Learning, when they asked me to do a new series of real estate letters for *5 Minutes to More Great Real Estate Letters.* I continue to get e-mails to this day from people thanking me for the letters in *5 Minutes to a Great Real Estate Letter,* and nothing is more satisfying than to receive nice and kind compliments about your work from your business colleagues. Thank you!

I would also like to thank all my good friends at Cengage Learning including Dave Shaut, Sara Glassmeyer, Mark Linton, Bud Hunsucker, and many others working behind the scenes at this fine company. Thank you to my editor, Arlin Kauffman, and to everyone in post-production for the book.

Thank you to all of my friends at the Council of Real Estate Brokerage Managers, Ginny Shipe and Kristin Carey, Terry Murphy (my good friend) at The Missouri Association of REALTORS®, and all of my past students, friends, and colleagues who have encouraged and helped me during my real estate career.

Of course, I appreciate and say thank you to my two daughters, Alyx and Anne, two of the finest daughters a dad could have! Thanks to my mom, Pat Mayfield, for introducing me to the field of real estate some 32 years ago.

And finally, a special thanks to my lovely wife, Kerry, whom I am so indebted to for all of her love and support. Without you, Kerry, this would not be possible.

HOW TO USE THIS BOOK

With *5 Minutes to More Great Real Estate Letters,* you will be able to incorporate your letters with Microsoft Word or Outlook. However, you do not need to have the software products to use the letters on this CD-ROM. I have also included the .txt files that you can import into whatever word processing program that you use, as most software allow for this feature. Many word processing programs will also open up a Microsoft Word document, so either option should be sufficient for you when using the letters from this book. As a reminder, if you do choose to use the .txt files, you will need to change the formatting, pick a different font, and make a few other changes so the letters look more professional. You can watch a short video on how to do this which is included on the CD-ROM.

Almost all of the letters throughout the book will require some customization and personalization on your part. Those letters will need your manual input to make the letters work properly. Below is an example:

> *"For a free price evaluation of what your property is worth in today's market, call me at [Agent Phone Number]. There are no high-pressure tactics and no obligation to list your house.*

In the above example, you will need to add your phone number to the paragraph for the letter to be ready for mailing. Once you make the necessary changes and save your letter to your computer's hard drive, it is ready for reuse to other clients without this extra step. Again, I included a short video that will help you understand how to use this book and save yourself a lot of time. I encourage you to watch the video on the enclosed CD-ROM.

Many of the fax/e-mail templates are designed for you to copy and paste into your fax template or e-mail message. These messages can save you time, especially if you incorporate some of these repeated tasks into an e-mail signature.

One final note, every attempt has been made to make the letters and videos on the CD-ROM match the step-by-step procedures currently used in Microsoft Office. If this information or keystrokes change with a new software upgrade by Microsoft, please check www.realestatetechguy.com to watch the latest videos for use with the letters and e-mail messages from the book. I will have these videos posted at my Web site under the resource tab.

I hope you enjoy the book and find it easy to use. I also hope it helps take your real estate career to a new level.

Sincerely,
John D. Mayfield

Prospecting

I once saw a church sign that had this phrase on it: "The only place where success comes before work is in the dictionary." If you want to have true success as a real estate professional, you MUST prospect! Prospecting is the core to developing and maintaining a profitable career. Prospecting does require work, and it does demand an unbroken chain of events. You cannot send one letter and expect fantastic results. Some potential clients may require four, five or more marketing pieces before they agree to do business with you. Unfortunately, many real estate agents fail to remind themselves of the importance of a continuous prospecting plan of action and will give up after only one attempt. A few others might make two contacts with the consumer, but most will quit after one or two tries. Prospecting is not a once a month "to do," or a "task" that is implemented when business begins to slow down but rather a daily "assignment" for every real estate professional. Today's real estate associate must make several attempts to secure new business.

There are many places and ways you can prospect, including your social networking groups and advertising for leads through Google, Yahoo and other Internet sites. And since this is a "letters" book, yes, you might even consider sending daily correspondence to consumers in your marketplace. *Five Minutes to More Great Real Estate Letters* is a resource book that will help you develop and maintain a continuous plan of action for your prospecting needs. As noted earlier, prospecting does require a little bit of work on your part, but with the letters included in the Prospecting section, as well as letters from *Five Minutes to a Great Real Estate Letter,* Cengage Learning and *Five Minutes to Great Marketing Ideas*, Cengage Learning, you will have more than enough marketing letters to win business for many years to come. However, if you want to become successful as a real estate professional, remember that ole' saying: "The only place where success comes before work is in the dictionary."

Prospecting to Apartments
One avenue often overlooked by many real estate agents is prospecting to local apartment complexes. The following letters are designed to help you target potential buyers who are residing in an apartment complex, yet long to have their own home. People choose to live in apartments for a number of reasons; therefore we have designed letters that address a number of these factors. The

key to apartment prospecting is "follow-up" and a continuous uninterrupted plan of action. You will find both initial introductory letters as well as follow-up correspondence you can use with your marketing efforts.

Remember, many apartment tenants have leases to fulfill, and a letter campaign that would exist over a six- to twelve-month time frame is ideal and will normally pay big dividends when followed through. One word of caution, don't overextend your letters to this prospecting group. Normally, a letter on a monthly basis or every other month is sufficient for this type of campaign. Also, never leave letters at the door in an apartment complex. This can be very upsetting to property managers and owners, and it is strongly advised that you send these letters through the U.S. Postal Service, or through e-mail.

Letters To Apartment Tenants

[Date]

«AddressBlock»

«GreetingLine»

Now is a GREAT time to buy. Interest rates are at an all-time low, and housing prices have never been more affordable. If you've been putting off the decision about buying a new home, you may want to reconsider. Hi, my name is (*AGENT NAME*), a real estate professional in (*CITY*). I have a good friend who is also a mortgage loan officer for (*NAME OF LENDER*) and has helped provide many of my clients with affordable home loans in the last few months. He would be happy to prequalify you (no charge for prequalification) and determine if you might qualify for one of his company's new loan products. If this is something you may have an interest in, please call or write me today and see if you may be able to take advantage of today's low interest rates and affordable housing prices.

If you are not in the market to purchase a new home but know of someone who is, I would truly appreciate you passing along my enclosed business card to them. Of course, the same offer would apply.

Thank you for your time, and I look forward to hearing from you soon.

Yours truly,

[Agent Name]
[Agent Title]

Letters To Apartment Tenants

[Date]

«AddressBlock»

«GreetingLine»

Over the last few years the real estate industry has witnessed some trying and difficult times in many individuals' lives. With record foreclosures and massive layoffs, a lot of people I have come into contact with today are having difficulties purchasing a home. True, bad credit can sometimes be a deterrent to purchasing a home; however, figuring out and knowing what you need to do to improve your credit score is an important first step in becoming a homeowner again. If this is something you are facing, I would love to assist in helping you own your own home once again.

I have a good friend and loan officer willing to meet with my customers, run updated credit reports, and help determine what steps could be taken to improve these credit scores. This is done completely confidentially and costs you absolutely nothing.

If you feel that this is something you would want to pursue and sounds interesting to you, please contact me at (*AGENT PHONE NUMBER*), and I can arrange an appointment for you to meet with her.

I appreciate your time, and please understand that these letters were sent randomly to this apartment complex. Your situation may not be in the manner as described in this letter, and you may only need to get preapproved for a loan. If so, please disregard the insinuation or notion that everyone who receives this is having credit difficulty.

I hope you sense my aspiration and will to be available for anyone who may need help or has a desire to own a home once again. If I can help you or any of your friends in any way, regardless of your credit situation, please feel free to give me a call.

I appreciate your time and hope to hear from you soon.

Yours truly,

[Agent Name]
[Agent Title]

Letters To Apartment Tenants

[Date]

«AddressBlock»

«GreetingLine»

Hello, my name is (*AGENT NAME*) from (*COMPANY NAME*). This letter is intended for everyone at (*APARTMENT COMPLEX NAME*). First, I realize there are many people who want, enjoy, and appreciate the opportunity to live in apartment housing. I understand and admire your decision and do not want this letter to be misinterpreted in any way. However, many of my past buyers have come directly out of apartment complexes. Therefore, sending letters in search of potential buyers is a good way for me to look for new business.

If you've ever thought about owning your own home, or would like to own a new home, I would love to help you. Today is a GREAT time to own your own home! With low interest rates and affordable housing prices, you really cannot go wrong by looking for your own home today. If this is something that you may be interested in, please feel free to contact me for a FREE consultation on how much home you could purchase in today's market.

You can reach me at (*AGENT PHONE NUMBER*) or e-mail me at (*AGENT E-MAIL*) for more information. Thank you for your time, and if you do not have an interest in this offer, please feel free to pass along my card to someone you may know who does.

I appreciate your time and hope to hear from you soon.

Yours truly,

[Agent Name]
[Agent Title]

Letters To Apartment Tenants

[Date]

«AddressBlock»

«GreetingLine»

Many satisfied homebuyers today once lived in an apartment like you currently do. Unfortunately, a large number of these new homebuyers believed that they could not qualify for a home loan. The reality is, interest rates are still low, and housing prices are still affordable.

Would you like to see how much home you qualify to buy on today's real estate market? This process is relatively quick and it is free. My friend (*MORTGAGE OFFICER NAME*), who is a loan officer in our area, has helped many people accomplish the dream of owning their own home. In just a few short minutes, (*MORTGAGE OFFICER NAME*) can help you discover how much you can afford and what type of loan will best suit your needs. There are many programs available that offer low down payments and other options for loan paybacks that might surprise you.

If you would like to discover if homeownership can be a reality for you in the next few months, please call me today at (*AGENT PHONE NUMBER*) to speak directly to me.

Please know that there is no obligation to purchase and that this is all totally free.

I would love to help you with your next home purchase, and I look forward to hearing from you soon.

Yours truly,

[Agent Name]
[Agent Title]

Letters To Apartment Tenants

[Date]

«AddressBlock»

«GreetingLine»

How much money are you willing to throw out the window?

I don't mean to be blunt, but did you realize that if a person pays $1,000 per month in rent, after a short 12-month period they would have thrown $12,000 out the window? That's right; the money you spend on rent will never be recovered and is gone forever. The opposite is normally true for people who purchase a home. Each month you make a payment, there is small portion that goes toward your principal value, not to mention the increased equity that your home can build over time due to increased price values. True, our economy can go up and down, and we have seen years when housing prices have fallen; however, in looking at the long term view of our nation's history, most homeowners have always done well by owning their own home.

Today there are some great buys in our real estate market, and interest rates are still very attractive. When you couple all this together, it provides the perfect climate for homeownership. Rather than watching you throw your hard earned money out the window each month, I would love to see you consider taking the first step toward homeownership. That step would be to determine how much you can afford, what's available, and what your proposed monthly payment would be if you were to begin looking at homes in the near future. There's no cost involved with this first step, and you also have my promise and pledge that there will be no high pressure on my end to get you to look at homes.

I want you to know that I am here to help and assist if homeownership is something you desire.

Please feel free to contact me at (*AGENT PHONE NUMBER*). I appreciate your time and I look forward to hearing from you soon.

Yours truly,

[Agent Name]
[Agent Title]

Prospecting

Letters To Apartment Tenants

[Date]

«AddressBlock»

«GreetingLine»

For many people, apartment living is an added plus, and they enjoy the benefits of living in this type of community. For others, the cramped quarters and the excessive noise can sometimes be too much to bear on a daily basis. For these folks, I want you to know there are options and opportunities to purchase your own home. If you have a desire to purchase your own home and experience your own quiet and comfortable surroundings, I can help. I enjoy specializing in serving apartment tenants and helping them find affordable housing.

I have a friend who is a mortgage loan officer who can assist us in taking the first steps into moving you into your new home.

Please contact me at (*AGENT PHONE NUMBER*) so that we can begin your journey to homeownership.

I appreciate your time and look forward to hearing from you soon.

Yours truly,

[Agent Name]
[Agent Title]

Letters To Apartment Tenants

[Date]

«AddressBlock»

«GreetingLine»

Many buyers are taking advantage of the low interest rates and attractive home prices by subscribing to my monthly newsletter. My newsletter contains tips for buying a home, as well as some of the best buys in our marketplace. I'd love to add you to my e-newsletter list; it's free, and I think you will find a wealth of information each month.

Each month you will receive new tips like this one: *How buyers are taking advantage of the HUD 203 (K) home loans on some of the foreclosed properties that need many improvements. The HUD 203 (K) loan will allow you to borrow extra money to help make the repairs on these discounted foreclosed homes.*

To sign up for my FREE e-newsletter designed especially for buyers, send an e-mail to (*AGENT E-MAIL*). I'll be sure to add you to my list, and don't worry, I never share or sell any of my names and e-mail addresses to anyone.

Become an informed buyer before you enter the marketplace, subscribe to my FREE e-newsletter today.

If you're ready to find out just how much home you will qualify for and are ready to get preapproved, call me, (*AGENT PHONE NUMBER*), to schedule your appointment today.

I appreciate your time, and I hope to hear from you soon.

Yours truly,

[Agent Name]
[Agent Title]

Letters To Apartment Tenants

[Date]

«AddressBlock»

«GreetingLine»

Have you ever thought about purchasing a home? If so, I would love to help you find your next home. True, homeownership can be a complicated process. I have developed an interactive CD-ROM entitled *Your Guide to Buying a New Home*. This is a virtual homebuyers workshop that you can watch from the comfort of your own home 24/7, 365 days a year, and contains some valuable information and advice to help you with purchasing a new home. This CD-ROM is free, and helps guide you through the necessary steps as a homebuyer.

Now is a GREAT time to purchase a home, and I would love to help you with the process. To receive your free copy simply call or e-mail me and request my interactive CD-ROM *Your Guide to Buying a New Home*. I'll be happy to deliver this in person or send it via U.S. Postal Service, whichever you prefer.

Please know there is no obligation to purchase your next home through me in requesting this free homebuyer's CD-ROM.

Yours truly,

[Agent Name]
[Agent Title]

Note to reader. You might consider putting together a handbook or guide to offer to apartment tenants if you do not have access to a CD-ROM program as noted in this letter. You may also visit www.RealEstateTechGuy.com for more information on ordering a customized copy of this CD-ROM for you or your company.

Follow-Up Letters
To Apartment Tenants

[Date]

«AddressBlock»

«GreetingLine»

I hope you received my letter recently about the opportunity to become "preapproved" for a home loan from my friend and loan officer (*MORTGAGE LOAN OFFICER*) with (*MORTGAGE COMPANY*). Our response has been overwhelming from our initial offer, and we wanted to make certain everyone had an opportunity to take advantage of this program. If you were not able to contact (*MORTGAGE OFFICER*) about this prequalification, please do so today. Interest rates and housing values are still at all-time lows, and this is the perfect time to invest in a home.

Many buyers are taking advantage of the HUD 203 (K) home loans on some of the foreclosed properties that need many improvements. The HUD 203 (K) loan will allow you to borrow extra money to help make the repairs on these discounted foreclosed homes.

Don't put off buying that new home any longer, today is the day to get preapproved to find out just how much home you will qualify for. Call me, (*AGENT PHONE NUMBER*), to schedule your appointment today.

I appreciate your time, and I hope to hear from you soon.

Yours truly,

[Agent Name]
[Agent Title]

Follow-Up Letters
To Apartment Tenants

[Date]

«AddressBlock»

«GreetingLine»

I hope you received my letter recently about the opportunity to become "preapproved" for a home loan from my friend and loan officer (*MORTGAGE LOAN OFFICER*) with (*MORTGAGE COMPANY*). Interest rates and housing values are still at all-time lows, and this is the perfect time to invest in a home.

Many buyers are taking advantage of the lowered prices on many foreclosed homes in our area. If this sounds interesting to you, I can set up a customized search in our local Multiple Listing Service to monitor homes that match what you're looking for. Once a new home in your price range and area becomes available, you'll be one of the first to find out about it. It's easy, it's FREE and it only takes me a couple of minutes to set up.

Be the first to find out about that next great deal in your city by calling me, (*AGENT PHONE NUMBER*), to set up your customized home search in our Multiple Listing Service today!

I appreciate your time, and I hope to hear from you soon.

Yours truly,

[Agent Name]
[Agent Title]

Follow-Up Letters
To Apartment Tenants

[Date]

«AddressBlock»

«GreetingLine»

I hope you received my letter recently about the opportunity to purchase a new home. Now is an excellent time to purchase a home, and housing prices and interest rates could not be better.

Don't put off buying that new home any longer, today is the day to get preapproved to find out just how much home you will qualify for. Call me, (*AGENT PHONE NUMBER*), to schedule a free home-buying consultation today.

I appreciate your time, and I hope to hear from you soon.

Yours truly,

[Agent Name]
[Agent Title]

Follow-Up Letters To Apartment Tenants

[Date]

«AddressBlock»

«GreetingLine»

I hope you received my letter recently about the opportunity to become a homeowner. Many buyers are taking advantage of the low interest rates and attractive home prices by subscribing to my monthly newsletter. My newsletter contains tips for buying a home, as well as some of the best buys in our marketplace. I'd love to add you to my e-newsletter list; it's free, and I think you will find a wealth of information each month.

Each month you will receive new tips like this one: *Many buyers are taking advantage of the HUD 203 (K) home loans on some of the foreclosed properties that need many improvements. The HUD 203 (K) loan will allow you to borrow extra money to help make the repairs on these discounted foreclosed homes.*

To sign up for my FREE e-newsletter designed especially for buyers, send an e-mail to (*AGENT E-MAIL*). I'll be sure to add you to my list, and don't worry, I never share or sell any of my names and e-mail addresses to anyone.

Become an informed buyer before you enter the marketplace, subscribe to my FREE e-newsletter today.

If you're ready to find out just how much home you will qualify for and ready to get preapproved, call me, (*AGENT PHONE NUMBER*), to schedule your appointment today.

I appreciate your time, and I hope to hear from you soon.

Yours truly,

[Agent Name]
[Agent Title]

Note, this letter will require you to commit to offering a monthly e-newsletter with tips and facts for homebuyers. Although this will require additional work, it is a great way to obtain e-mail addresses from potential buyers and to easily communicate with them in the future.

E-Mail Or Follow-Up Letters In Response To Your Letters

[Date]

«AddressBlock»

«GreetingLine»

Thank you for responding to my request about the opportunity to assist you in buying your own home. I am in the process of having my good friend (*MORTGAGE LOAN OFFICER*) contact you about the necessary information he will need to begin the process. In the meantime, let me know if you have any additional questions, and I will contact you soon.

Thanks again for responding to my offer!

Yours truly,

[Agent Name]
[Agent Title]

Note, this letter will require you to commit to offering a monthly e-newsletter with tips and facts for homebuyers. Although this will require additional work, it is a great way to obtain e-mail addresses from potential buyers and to easily communicate with them in the future.

E-Mail Or Follow-Up Letters In Response To Your Letters

[Date]

«AddressBlock»

«GreetingLine»

Thank you for your recent request about buying your own home. As promised, I have contacted (*MORTGAGE LOAN OFFICER*) to get in touch with you regarding the necessary steps we discussed by telephone, to help him determine how much you qualify for. Please let me know if you do not hear from him, and I will make sure and follow-up.

Otherwise, we'll be in touch and determine our next steps once you've met with (*MORTGAGE LOAN OFFICER*).

Thanks again for contacting me, and I look forward to helping you find your next home.

Yours truly,

[Agent Name]
[Agent Title]

For Sale by Owner (FSBO) Letters

Letters To For Sale By Owners

[Date]

«AddressBlock»

«GreetingLine»

I was driving through your neighborhood today and noticed your house listed for sale by owner. Congratulations on your marketing endeavors, and I hope that you've found some success during the marketing of your property. I understand why many people attempt to market properties on their own; however, there are several things that I'd like every for sale by owner to be aware of.

On my Web site (*COMPANY WEB ADDRESS*), under the tab "Sellers Information", you will find a link to a video I have created entitled *What Every for Sale by Owner Should Know.* I would encourage you to check out my Web site, especially the video I've prepared for consumers like you who are selling their property on their own. It's an educational and informative video on some things that you definitely must consider and do while selling your property on your own. The video is not very long, but is filled with information that can help you save thousands of dollars, plus provides you with many safety measures you should undertake when meeting perspective customers.

If you'd like to visit with me and learn more about my services and some of the things I do for my current clients, feel free to call me or write me. I've enclosed my business card for reference should you need to contact me.

Thank you for your time, and I hope to hear from you soon.

Yours truly,

[Agent Name]
[Agent Title]

Letters To For Sale By Owners

[Date]

«AddressBlock»

«GreetingLine»

In driving through your neighborhood, I noticed that you have your house for sale by owner. I realize many sellers like to test the waters and see if they might be able to sell their home on their own. There is nothing wrong with self-marketing your property, and sometimes it can be a positive experience. However, most homes today are sold through the Multiple Listing Service (MLS). Most buyers who are working with real estate agents use the MLS to locate which properties are for sale in (*MARKET AREA*). If your home is not listed in the MLS, then you're missing out on many potential prospects.

The bottom line is this: whether your house is listed with my company or another company, it is important to have your home listed in the MLS. It plays a vital role in how properties are sold in today's real estate market.

Virtual tours, property placement in online classifieds sites, along with many other internet techniques to help sell properties today also play a big part in real estate marketing. If you would have an interest in learning more about marketing ideas I can provide you for selling your property, please feel free to call or write me at: (*AGENT PHONE NUMBER*) or (*AGENT E-MAIL*).

Thank you for your time, best of luck with the marketing of your property and please do not hesitate to contact me if I can help answer any questions.

Yours truly,

[Agent Name]
[Agent Title]

Letters To For Sale By Owners—(Follow-Up Letter)

[Date]

«AddressBlock»

«GreetingLine»

Hope you received the letter I sent you last week about your property for sale. When I was driving by today, I noticed that you are still trying to sell on your own. If you have not found a buyer yet, I have a couple of ideas I'd like to share with you that you can do on your own, or I would be happy to help you with.

For a FREE, no pressure to list consultation please call me at (*AGENT PHONE NUMBER*). I would love to visit with you about some of these free marketing ideas that I can help put together for you.

Thanks for your time, and I hope to hear from you soon.

Yours truly,

[Agent Name]
[Agent Title]

Letters To For Sale By Owners—(Follow-Up Letter)

[Date]

«AddressBlock»

«GreetingLine»

I noticed your house is still for sale by owner. I don't mean to be a pest, but I love helping people like you with their real estate needs. Yes, sometimes if I can provide buyers and sellers with helpful information, it allows them to get to know me a little better, and many times it leads to new friendships and the possibility for future business.

Today while I was in your neighborhood I took a picture of your house and embedded it into a sample flyer template that we use at our office to promote and market houses that we sell. I would be happy to provide you with a few of these free flyers, as well as a flyer box to put in front of your house if this is something you have an interest in. You can reach me at (*AGENT PHONE NUMBER*), and I will be happy to collect additional details about your home for the flyer and discuss what you would want on the flyer. Please understand that my initial copying of ten flyers is free of charge. You may then take the template to a copy store to have additional copies made if you desire.

If this offer sounds interesting to you, please contact me, and I will get to work immediately on this project for you.

Yours truly,

[Agent Name]
[Agent Title]

Letters To For Sale By Owners—(Follow-Up Letter)

[Date]

«AddressBlock»

«GreetingLine»

I noticed your house is still for sale. I was just curious if you had put a virtual tour of your home on YouTube? Many real estate agents have had good success by putting their properties on YouTube. Consumers love to look at pictures and videos of properties today and there are several easy ways that you can create videos to host on this popular Web site.

If you need some help in producing a short video for YouTube about your property, I'd be glad to help you at no additional charge. It's my way of introducing myself and helping you get ready to list with a real estate agent. There's no cost or obligation to list with me helping you with the video.

If this offer is of interest to you, please contact me at (*AGENT PHONE NUMBER*) or (*E-MAIL*).

Thanks for your time, and I hope to hear from you soon.

Yours truly,

[Agent Name]
[Agent Title]

E-Mail Or Follow-Up Letters In Response To Your Letters

[Date]

«AddressBlock»

«GreetingLine»

Thank you for responding to my request about the opportunity to be pre-approved for a home loan. I will have someone contact you shortly to help you with this offer.

Thanks again for responding to my offer, and I look forward to working with you on purchasing your next home!

Yours truly,

[Agent Name]
[Agent Title]

E-Mail Or Follow-Up Letters In Response To Your Letters

[Date]

«AddressBlock»

«GreetingLine»

Thank you for your recent request about the opportunity to receive my FREE information on how to purchase a home. I will have this information sent to you immediately. Please don't hesitate to call if you have any questions you need answered from the material I will be forwarding to you.

Thanks again for contacting me, and I look forward to helping you find your next home.

Yours truly,

[Agent Name]
[Agent Title]

Prospecting— Expired Listings

[Date]

«AddressBlock»

«GreetingLine»

As I was searching through our Multiple Listing Service (MLS) today I noticed that your house had recently expired. I am sure you understand that since your listing has expired it is no longer available to potential homebuyers through the MLS Web site, REALTOR.com, and many other online listing portals. Don't get discouraged that your property did not sell; it might just mean that you need a fresh new beginning to jumpstart your marketing activity.

At (*COMPANY NAME*) we offer a wide variety of innovative marketing ideas to help sell properties quickly. I would love to visit with you to further some of our ways to help sell your property.

Please feel free to call me at (*AGENT PHONE NUMBER*) to set up your FREE consultation on how we can get the most for your property.

Yours truly,

[Agent Name]
[Agent Title]

Prospecting—Expired Listings

[Date]

«AddressBlock»

«GreetingLine»

I noticed that your property expired today in our Multiple Listing Service. Unfortunately the expiration of your listing also means that all marketing activities must stop. If you do not want your listing advertising to cease, I would be happy to discuss some of my innovative and successful marketing ideas with you.

Sometimes a change of pace and a fresh new yard sign can make all the difference in the world!

If you would like to find out more about myself and (*COMPANY NAME*), and what our marketing efforts can do for you, please contact me at (*AGENT PHONE NUMBER*)

Thanks for your time, and I hope to hear from you soon.

Yours truly,

[Agent Name]
[Agent Title]

Prospecting—
Expired Listings

[Date]

«AddressBlock»

«GreetingLine»

Your house has officially been off the market for one week. I realize you have probably been bombarded with many phone calls and letters from other real estate agencies inquiring about your listing. At (*COMPANY NAME*) we offer some exciting new Internet marketing procedures for each and every listing we take. If you're still in the market to sell your property, I would love to visit with you and share some of our new ideas about how to get top dollar for your property.

Now is still an excellent time to sell your property even though you weren't successful with your previous attempt. Let's meet so I can share with you some new ways to get your property sold soon.

I look forward to hearing from you, and my business card is enclosed for you to contact me.

Yours truly,

[Agent Name]
[Agent Title]

Prospecting— Expired Listings

[Date]

«AddressBlock»

«GreetingLine»

I hope you have received the previous letters I sent you over the last few weeks? I noticed your property is still showing expired in our Multiple Listing Service, (MLS). I spent some time reviewing the information about your property in our MLS, and it looks like your previous agent did a thorough job with the listing remarks. I was curious if your previous real estate agent utilized some of the new online marketing programs to promote your property? Today there are many online listing Web sites where properties can be published to attract a larger buying audience. I am proud to say that at (COMPANY NAME) we use many of these Web sites to promote and market our listings for sale.

If you feel your property was not adequately listed on some of the online classified sites, I would love to visit with you and share some of the methods we use to find real estate buyers. These sources have become golden opportunities for our agency to sell properties. We also use many other Internet marketing ideas such as YouTube, Flickr and other social networking Web sites to help promote our real estate listings.

I feel certain you would be pleased with my services, and I would love to visit with you to further some of these exciting Internet marketing procedures I have.

Please feel free to contact me at your earliest convenience. You can reach me at (AGENT PHONE NUMBER). I appreciate your time, and I look forward to hearing from you soon.

Yours truly,

[Agent Name]
[Agent Title]

Prospecting— Expired Listings

[Date]

«AddressBlock»

«GreetingLine»

Yes, it's your friendly real estate pest. Actually, I hope that I'm not becoming a pest by writing you so often with regards to your expired listing from our Multiple Listing Service. I do hope you can witness and appreciate my willingness to follow-up and stay on top of my real estate activities. Naturally, if you had a prospective buyer on your property you would want someone like me who would stay on top of the situation and follow through with any potential buyers.

If you're still thinking about putting your house back up for sale, I would love to visit with you. Please feel free to contact me at (*AGNET PHONE NUMBER*) at your earliest convenience. I have some exciting marketing plans and ideas on how we can get top dollar for your real estate.

I do appreciate your time, and I look forward to hearing from you soon.

Yours truly,

[Agent Name]
[Agent Title]

Prospecting— Expired Listings

[Date]

«AddressBlock»

«GreetingLine»

One of the things I pride myself on is a continuous and consistent follow-up with my listing clients. I realize that good communication with my clients is essential to getting the property sold. Regular updates on the marketing activities, feedback from showings, and general phone calls to discuss the property with my clients are all things that help lead to a successful real estate transaction.

If you're looking for a real estate professional who can stay in touch, monitor all aspects of the real estate marketing, and keep you informed of all these activities, then we need to talk. I would love to show you my game plan and ideas to help get your property sold!

I appreciate your time in reading my letter, and I do hope we can visit soon.

Yours truly,

[Agent Name]
[Agent Title]

Prospecting—
Expired Listings

[Date]

«AddressBlock»

«GreetingLine»

Still Curious Why Your House Did Not Sell?

I understand that your house has been listed on the market and did not sell. Normally, there are two main reasons that your house did not sell.

1. Your house was overpriced
2. The economic climate

Sometimes it's easy to blame a real estate agent, company or many other issues, but the cold hard facts boil down to those two facts noted above.

The first question you need to ask yourself, *"Is our house really worth what we're asking for it?"* A detailed price evaluation about what's happening in the marketplace can normally answer this question. If your agent did not provide you with a written market evaluation on what your property is worth, then perhaps this is a good starting point in determining why your house did not sell. I would be happy to assist in determining what your home is worth on today's real estate market. My evaluation will be a truthful, honest price evaluation with no fluff. If I can't sell your home for what it's worth, then it does neither one of us any good to place it on the market at an inflated price.

If you would like to find out more, please contact me at (*AGENT PHONE NUMBER*) to arrange a FREE consultation. I would be happy to help find out why your house did not sell, and provide you with my findings.

I appreciate your time, and I hope to hear from you soon.

Yours truly,

[Agent Name]
[Agent Title]

Prospecting— Expired Listings

[Date]

«AddressBlock»

«GreetingLine»

I was curious if your real estate agent provided you with a weekly real estate update? Unfortunately, many agents fail to understand the importance of communicating with their clients regularly. One of my major goals is to make certain my real estate clients receive a regular update about the marketing activities on their home sale. Good communication can help make the home-selling process much easier.

As I've mentioned in my previous letters, I have some exciting and great marketing ideas I would love to share with you about how we might get the maximum exposure to potential buyers on your property.

If you would like to discover my business plan for helping expired listings get a jumpstart on their next introduction to the marketplace, please call me. I have included my business card for you to contact me to arrange for a private consultation.

As always, "thank you" for your time, and I hope to hear from you soon.

Yours truly,

[Agent Name]
[Agent Title]

Prospecting—
Expired Listings

[Date]

«AddressBlock»

«GreetingLine»

One of the questions I hear from many expired listing clients is whether or not they should take their home off the market for a while when it does not sell the first or second time. My feeling is that it's normally better to keep a continuous marketing effort in place. Taking your property off the market can possibly make you miss out on many potential buyers. There are some drawbacks to leaving your property on the market for an extended period of time, but in the long run you will be much better off pricing your property correctly, and leaving it exposed to the marketplace.

There are many items like this I would be happy to discuss with you if you are still interested in selling. I have enclosed my business card for you to contact me if you would like to schedule a FREE consultation on why your home probably did not sell.

As always, I want to thank you for your time for reading my letter, and I hope to hear from you soon.

Yours truly,

[Agent Name]
[Agent Title]

Prospecting— Expired Listings

[Date]

«AddressBlock»

«GreetingLine»

Where Do Buyers Come From?

For most home sellers, understanding where potential buyers come from is a topic that is never discussed with their real estate agent, yet it's an important piece of marketing information you should know. According to the most recent research from the National Association of REALTORS®, most buyers today come from the Internet. Now that your home has been off the market for several weeks, the potential exposure to buyers has disappeared since it is no longer on the World Wide Web. It you're still interested in selling your house, I believe placing your property for sale once again where it can be listed in the Multiple Listing Service along with various Web sites would be a plus. At (*COMPANY NAME*) we provide our clients with a large list of Internet sites we use to promote our listings.

I'm still eager to meet and visit with you and discuss your real estate needs when you're ready to sell your property. As always, thank you for your time for reading my letter, and I hope to hear from you soon.

Yours truly,

[Agent Name]
[Agent Title]

Prospecting— Expired Listings

[Date]

«AddressBlock»

«GreetingLine»

I realize the road to selling a home can be a long and trying process. At (*COMPANY NAME*) our goal is to help make the home-selling process as easy as possible, and we have developed several tips and a business plan to help accomplish this.

Our first step in our business plan to sell your property is to provide you with a detailed price evaluation on what we believe your home is worth on today's market. It's important that we provide you with accurate and honest information on what we think your home will sell for. After all, it profits no one to place a home on the market that is priced too high.

Another area that we try and do at (*COMPANY NAME*) is to assist you in providing suggestions on things you should change to help merchandise your home better. Sometimes these suggestions could require painting and cleaning, moving or eliminating excess furniture.

These are just two items that can help streamline the home-selling process and make the road much easier for everyone involved. It is difficult to convey these items and more through written correspondence; however, I would be more than happy to meet with you in person and discuss some ideas that may help generate a successful SOLD sign for your property. I've enclosed a business card for you to contact me to arrange your initial consultation.

Thanks again for your time, and I do look forward to hearing from you soon.

Yours truly,

[Agent Name]
[Agent Title]

Prospecting— Expired Listings

[Date]

«AddressBlock»

«GreetingLine»

I have a seven-point checklist that I ask every expired listing client who chooses me as their real estate professional.

1. Did your agent provide you with a written price evaluation on your property?
2. Did your agent provide you with suggestions and ideas to improve the salability of your property?
3. Did your agent plan out a 60-day marketing activity sheet with your input?
4. Did your agent provide you a list of Web sites your house would be featured on?
5. Did your agent send "Just Listed" letters and brochures to your neighborhood?
6. Did your agent set up an agent open house during the first two weeks?
7. Did your agent send you regular marketing status reports?

These are just a few of the services you will find that I provide my clients when they choose to list their property with me. I have some excellent new marketing ideas and plans I would love to share with you on how I have helped other expired listing clients sell their homes.

If you would like to know more about how I am a different real estate professional than the average agent, please call me at (*AGENT PHONE NUMBER*). I would love to help you get your property sold in as fast a time frame as possible.

Call me so that we may schedule an appointment that works well for both of us. If you prefer to contact me by e-mail, please send your request to (*AGENT E-MAIL*). Also, you may text message my cell phone if you prefer to use this method of communication.

Thanks for your time, and I look forward to hearing from you soon.

Yours truly,

[Agent Name]
[Agent Title]

Prospecting—
Expired Listings

[Date]

«AddressBlock»

«GreetingLine»

I realize it has been several weeks since you had your property for sale in our local real estate market. I have sent you a few letters over the last few months, and I appreciate the fact that you have not called or been upset with my continuous follow through. As I mentioned several letters back, following up on leads and keeping my clients informed on my marketing activity is an important part of my business. I realized a long time ago how important a systematic plan of action to stay in touch with my clients and prospects is. Good communication is positive and beneficial for everyone involved.

I understand that there may be several factors on why you have not reentered the real estate market, but rest assured that you can count on me for timely, accurate information on how to sell your property today.

I am eager and ready for your business and have enclosed a business card for you to contact me if you still have a desire to sell your property. You're welcome to contact me on my mobile phone number.

Thank you for your time, and I look forward to hearing from you soon.

Yours truly,

[Agent Name]
[Agent Title]

Farm Area Letters

Letters To Farm Area

[Date]

«AddressBlock»

«GreetingLine»

How to get top dollar out of your real estate
Did you know there are several things you should do to get top dollar from your real estate, regardless of any economic condition? I've included two tips for you to consider below from my FREE report, *"How to Save Thousands on Your Next Home Sale."*

■ When you're ready to begin showing your house to prospective buyers, remember to open the drapes and turn on the lights. It is always a good idea to allow as much light into your property as possible. Turning on lights; adding new, stronger light bulbs; and opening blinds and drapes is a big plus for marketing your property.

■ Keep copies of receipts on items you have purchased over the last couple of years. This can be helpful to potential homebuyers to verify and know how much money you have invested in your real estate on an annual basis.

These are just two suggestions that can help you when and if you are planning to sell. If you would like the full report on how to get top dollar when you sell your home, feel free to call me at (*AGENT PHONE NUMBER*) or (*AGENT E-MAIL*) for my full FREE report on how to save thousands the next time you sell a home.

Yours truly,

[Agent Name]
[Agent Title]

Note: If you prefer to offer this as a free report on your Web site, you can change the letter accordingly and direct consumers to your Web site for downloading this free report. Also, you can obtain copies of many FREE reports from 5 Minutes to Great Real Estate Marketing Ideas, Cengage Learning from any bookstore or www. RealEstateTechGuy.com

Letters To Farm Area

[Date]

«AddressBlock»

«GreetingLine»

As a real estate professional for (*COMPANY NAME*), I have realized what a great subdivision (*SUBDIVISION NAME*) is, and how well the properties sell in your area. I have decided to make your subdivision a focal point in my expertise and to specialize in listing and selling properties in this market area. To kick off my new marketing endeavors, I have created a special report on real estate activity in (*SUBDIVISION NAME*) and would be happy to share this FREE report with you.

You may request a copy of my (*SUBDIVISION NAME*) marketing report by e-mailing me at (*AGENT E-MAIL*) or calling me at (*AGENT PHONE NUMBER*). Each edition contains information about what properties have sold or that have recently gone on the market for sale. Again, the report is FREE, and I believe you will find it a valuable reference to have.

Please note, if you can provide me with your e-mail address, I will be happy to forward the (*SUBDIVISION NAME*) marketing report to you as I produce it. By subscribing to my report, you will know and remain knowledgeable in what's happening in (*SUBDIVISION NAME*).

Thanks for your time, and let me know if I can help you with any of your future real estate needs.

Yours truly,

[Agent Name]
[Agent Title]

P.S. All e-mail addresses added to my list are NEVER sold or shared with anyone else. Thanks!

Letters To Farm Area

[Date]

«AddressBlock»

«GreetingLine»

I'm excited to share my new real estate report for (*SUBDIVISION NAME*). Each month I'll be providing an updated report as to all the activity that is taking place with regards to real estate in (*SUBDIVISION NAME*). If you would like to subscribe to this FREE report and receive it each month via e-mail, simply send an e-mail to (*AGENT E-MAIL*) and insert subject line: (*SUBDIVISION NAME*) Report.

There's no obligation to buy or sell through me, and again, the report is FREE and will provide you with some valuable insight into the world of real estate in (*SUBDIVISION NAME*).

I look forward to providing you with your free report.

Yours truly,

[Agent Name]
[Agent Title]

PS. If you do not have an e-mail address and would like this FREE report mailed to you via the US Postal Service, please call me with your information, and I will be glad to add you to this list.

Letters To Farm Area

[Date]

«AddressBlock»

«GreetingLine»

Do you know…

- what the average sales price is for (*SUBDIVISION NAME*)?
- what the average days on market are for a home in (*SUBDIVISION NAME*)?
- what the list to sales price ratio is for (*SUBDIVISION NAME*)?
- how many homes have sold in (*SUBDIVISION NAME*)?

If not, I have some great news for you! Now, you can take advantage of receiving my valuable FREE marketing report about (*SUBDIVISION NAME*). Each month I'll recap the activity that's taking place in your subdivision and send it to you in a concise, easy to read format so that you will know exactly what's happening in (*SUBDIVISION NAME*). It's a great tool for you to gauge what your current real estate may be worth on today's real estate market. Although there are many variables that go into determining what your property is really worth on today's market, this FREE report can give you some basic insights as to what is going on in (*SUBDIVISION NAME*).

There are two ways you can receive this report, either through e-mail or through the US Postal Service. If you would like to receive it via e-mail, simply send an e-mail to me with subject line: (*SUBDIVISION NAME*) FREE report. If you do not have an e-mail address and prefer to receive it via US Postal Service, you may send me a note in the mail or call me at (*AGENT PHONE NUMBER*), and I'll be glad to add you to my list of registered homeowners who receive the hard copy version of my (*SUBDIVISION NAME*) marketing report.

I appreciate your time, and I hope that I can include you with the (*SUBDIVISION NAME*) real estate report.

Yours truly,

[Agent Name]
[Agent Title]

P.S. All e-mail addresses added to my list are NEVER sold or shared with anyone else. Thanks!

Letters To Farm Area

[Date]

«AddressBlock»

«GreetingLine»

Would you like to know what your property might bring in today's real estate market? For a FREE price evaluation (no obligation to list or sell), please feel free to call me at (*AGENT PHONE NUMBER*). I'll be happy to compare your property to homes that have sold in the last six months to determine an approximate list price that your house could bring in today's real estate market.

Again, there is no obligation to list or sell through me. This is your FREE opportunity to find out what one of the biggest investments you have may be worth in today's real estate market.

Thanks for your time. I hope to hear from you soon.

Yours truly,

[Agent Name]
[Agent Title]

Letters To Farm Area

[Date]

«AddressBlock»

«GreetingLine»

(SUBDIVISION NAME) is one of my favorite real estate subdivisions in all of *(AREA NAME)*. I am always thrilled to market properties in your area. Currently there is a shortage of listings in *(SUBDIVISION NAME)*. Because of this, I was writing to many folks who live in your neighborhood and inquiring as to whether you might have an interest in selling your property. If this is something you have been discussing or talking about and would like to know what your property might be worth, I would love to visit with you further. Please know that there is no obligation to list or sell, and I promise not to intrude too long on your time.

I've been helping families for *(YEARS OF EXPERIENCE)* and I would consider it an honor to help you with your next real estate transaction.

Again, thank you for your time, and I would love to hear from you soon.

Yours truly,

[Agent Name]
[Agent Title]

Note: For new real estate agents, you may substitute the length of time your company has been in business helping families instead of your personal time period.

Letters To Farm Area

[Date]

«AddressBlock»

«GreetingLine»

My name is (*AGENT NAME*); I'm a real estate agent with (*COMPANY NAME*) in (*CITY NAME*). Right now I'm looking for homes I might be able to sell in (*SUBDIVISION NAME*). If you or someone you might know in your neighborhood may have an interest in putting their property up for sale, I would love to hear from you. I have several innovative marketing ideas that can help you get top dollar for your real estate.

If this offer is of interest to you, you can reach me at (*AGENT PHONE NUMBER*) or (*AGENT E-MAIL*).

Thank you for your time, and I hope to hear from you soon.

Yours truly,

[Agent Name]
[Agent Title]

Letters To Farm Area

[Date]

«AddressBlock»

«GreetingLine»

Wanted: Real Estate Listings in (*SUBDIVISION NAME*)…

Due to a shortage of homes for sale in your neighborhood, I am currently looking for people who might have an interest in selling their real estate. If you, or if you know of someone who might have a desire to place their house for sale on today's market, please give me a call at (*AGENT PHONE NUMBER*). Our office has seen an influx of interest from buyers for (*SUBDIVISION NAME*), and we may be able to help you get top dollar for your real estate today.

For a FREE price evaluation on what your property might be worth today, call or e-mail me at (*AGENT PHONE NUMBER*), (*AGENT E-MAIL*). I would be happy to help you and provide you with research about what homes are selling for in (*SUBDIVISON NAME*). Please know that there is no obligation to list or sell through me or my company if you inquire about this FREE offer.

I appreciate your time, and I hope to hear from you soon.

Yours truly,

[Agent Name]
[Agent Title]

Letters To Farm Area

[Date]

«AddressBlock»

«GreetingLine»

THERE IS A DEMAND FOR HOMES IN (*SUBDIVISION NAME)*!

Yes, it's the old supply and demand theory; a low supply of inventory along with a high demand will drive prices to a maximum point. Currently in (*SUBDIVISION NAME*), there are very few homes for sale (low supply), along with an increased demand from buyers who want to live in your neighborhood. Both of these variables make the perfect recipe for what we call a "seller's market." That's right; it might be the perfect time for you to get top dollar for your real estate if you have a desire to sell.

If you have an interest in selling your home, I would love to talk to you and discuss how much your property might be worth in today's market. For a FREE price evaluation on what your property might be worth, call or e-mail me at (*AGENT PHONE NUMBER*), (*AGENT E-MAIL*). By the way, there is no obligation to list or sell through me or my company should you choose to take me up on my offer.

It would be an honor to help you with your real estate needs, and my initial consultation will only take a small amount of your time to discuss and share with you what your house may be worth on today's real estate market.

Thank you for taking time out to read my letter, and I look forward to hearing from you soon.

Yours truly,

[Agent Name]
[Agent Title]

Letters To Farm Area

[Date]

«AddressBlock»

«GreetingLine»

Yes, we've sold another one in (*SUBDIVISION OR CITY NAME*). Recently I closed on the property at (*SOLD PROPERTY ADDRESS*) in your neighborhood. The best part about this news is that there is still a large demand for properties in (*SUBDIVISION OR CITY NAME*).

If you have an interest in selling your property, I would love to talk to you about what the estimated value might be for your home. You can call me at (*AGENT PHONE NUMBER)* or reach me via e-mail at (*AGENT E-MAIL*) to schedule an appointment today. Please rest assured that there is no obligation to list or sell through me or my company with regards to this FREE offer to find out what your property might be worth in today's real estate market.

Thank you for your time, and I hope to hear from you soon.

Yours truly,

[Agent Name]
[Agent Title]

Letters To Farm Area

[Date]

«AddressBlock»

«GreetingLine»

I'm excited to announce that I recently participated in the closing in (*SUBDIVISION OR CITY NAME*). Right now there is still a large demand for properties in (*SUBDIVISION OR CITY NAME*), and it might be a good time to get top dollar for your real estate if you have an interest in selling.

I am currently offering FREE price evaluations on homes in (*SUBDIVISION OR CITY NAME*) for a limited time. If this is something that you would have an interest in exploring, please call me at (*AGENT PHONE NUMBER*) or reach me by e-mail at (*AGENT E-MAIL*) to schedule your FREE price evaluation appointment today.

I want to give you my pledge that there is no obligation to list or sell through me or my company with regards to this FREE offer, and I promise to respect your time during our initial consultation.

Thank you for taking time out to read my letter, and I hope to hear from you soon.

Yours truly,

[Agent Name]
[Agent Title]

Letters To Farm Area

[Date]

«AddressBlock»

«GreetingLine»

(*SUBDIVISION NAME*) has always been a great area to sell homes. I'm currently looking for homeowners in your subdivision who might be interested in selling their property. Now is an excellent time to get top dollar for your real estate, and I would love to show and explain some of the new innovative marketing services I offer my clients.

If this is something you may have an interest in knowing more about, please feel free to contact me at (*AGENT PHONE NUMBER*).

I appreciate your time and hope to hear from you soon.

Yours truly,

[Agent Name]
[Agent Title]

Letters To Farm Area

[Date]

«AddressBlock»

«GreetingLine»

You've probably already noticed that there are very few homes for sale in your subdivision. This one basic economic principle is a good indicator that you may able to get top dollar for your real estate. Any time when there is a lack of inventory for sale but there is a large demand for homes in a given location, it helps drive the housing prices up. Since this new trend has taken effect, many homeowners would like to know what the value of their current real estate investment is worth. If you have an interest in selling in the near future, I would be happy to offer you a FREE price evaluation and share with you my research on what your house might bring in today's real estate market. There is no obligation to list or sell through me or my company.

Please feel free to contact me at (*AGENT PHONE NUMBER*) so we can schedule an appointment that is convenient for you. I appreciate your time, and I look forward to hearing from you soon.

Yours truly,

[Agent Name]
[Agent Title]

Letters To Farm Area

[Date]

«AddressBlock»

«GreetingLine»

Are you looking for a bigger home with more room for your family? Now is a great time to take advantage of today's attractive real estate prices. If so, I can help! Hello, my name is (*AGENT NAME*) with (*COMPANY NAME*), and I am currently looking for new listings in (*SUBDIVISION OR CITY NAME*). I thought there may be a few people in your area looking to move up to a larger home or even downsize to a smaller home, who might be interested in selling. Either way, I would love to help you with your next real estate transaction.

If you have an interest in buying or selling real estate and want to know what is available in our marketplace, as well as what your home is worth on today's real estate market, please contact me at (*AGENT PHONE NUMBER*).

I appreciate your time, and I hope to hear from you soon.

Yours truly,

[Agent Name]
[Agent Title]

Letters To Farm Area

[Date]

«AddressBlock»

«GreetingLine»

As I was driving through (*SUBDIVISION NAME*) I could not help but notice how well kept the homes, lawns, and landscaping are in your area. People take great pride in homeownership in (*SUBDIVISION NAME*), and it really shows.

I wanted to send you a letter and include my business card and ask that you remember me when the time comes that you have an interest for real estate needs. I realize there are many qualified real estate agents to choose from; however, I feel that my company and I have some extra tools and services to offer over my competition when it comes to real estate marketing. If you would like to discuss some of our new innovative ways we implement to market real estate, and see what your home might bring in today's real estate market, I would love to visit with you further.

You may reach me at (*AGENT PHONE NUMBER*). Thanks again for your time, and I hope to hear from you soon.

Yours truly,

[Agent Name]
[Agent Title]

Letters To Farm Area

[Date]

«AddressBlock»

«GreetingLine»

I am currently working with some potential buyers who are looking for a property in (*subdivision name*) but unfortunately we have not been able to find the right property for them.

If you or someone you know in your neighborhood might have an interest in selling, I would love to visit with them further to discuss what my buyers are looking for. You can contact me at (*AGENT phone NUMBER*) or (*AGENT e-mail*).

There is no obligation to list your property, and my visit can help us both determine if my buyers might have an interest in your property. I appreciate your time, and I look forward to hearing from you soon.

Yours truly,

[Agent Name]
[Agent Title]

Just Listed In Your Neighborhood

[Date]

«AddressBlock»

«GreetingLine»

Recently I listed the property at [*Property Address*] for [*Owner's Name*]. This is a lovely home with many nice features and upgrades available. I was hopeful that you may know of someone interested in purchasing a home in your neighborhood and thought I would pass this information along to you.

The enclosed informational sheet will give you many details about this new listing along with the current asking price. I would appreciate any referrals you could provide me on this new listing, and if you know of someone I should contact directly, please feel free to let me know and I will reach out and call them personally.

I appreciate your time, and please let me know if I can be of help in any way with your real estate needs.

Yours truly,

[Agent Name]
[Agent Title]

Just Listed In Your Neighborhood

[Date]

«AddressBlock»

«GreetingLine»

I just listed the home at [*Property Address*] in your neighborhood. I have enclosed an informational sheet for you in case you have a friend or family member interested in relocating to your neighborhood. I can normally show this home on short notice, and I would love to help anyone you may know who might have an interest.

If you are thinking about buying or selling your home, I would love to help you and also provide you with a FREE price evaluation on what your property might be worth on today's real estate market.

Please contact me at [*Agent Phone Number*] or [*Agent E-Mail*], and I will be happy to schedule an appointment to meet you at your earliest convenience. There's no charge for this service, and I also promise no repeated phone calls or follow-up pressure tactics about listing your property.

I appreciate your time, and I look forward to hearing from you soon.

Yours truly,

[Agent Name]
[Agent Title]

Just Listed In Your Neighborhood

[Date]

«AddressBlock»

«GreetingLine»

Wow, I just listed [*Property Address*], and based on my research it appears to be an excellent buy! I wanted to write and tell you about the property just in case you knew of someone you would like to have as a new neighbor. I have enclosed an informational flyer for you and would appreciate any referrals you may be able to provide me regarding potential buyers in your neighborhood.

Thank you for your time, and please let me know if I can help you or any of your friends with their real estate needs.

Yours truly,

[Agent Name]
[Agent Title]

Just Listed In Your Neighborhood

[Date]

«AddressBlock»

«GreetingLine»

Hello, my name is [*Agent Name*], I am with [*Company Name*], and I am working with some buyers who are relocating to our area. They specifically like [*Subdivision Name*] and would love to make this area their new home. Unfortunately we have looked high and low for properties in [*Subdivision Name*] with no luck. I was taking this opportunity to write all of the homeowners in your subdivision to see if there was someone who may have an interest in selling. If so, please contact me as soon as possible at [*Agent Phone Number*] so we may discuss this matter more thoroughly.

Again, if you have an interest in selling, there may be a possibility I have a buyer. I would love to visit with you more, and I look forward to hearing from you soon.

Yours truly,

[Agent Name]
[Agent Title]

Just Sold House In Neighborhood—Letter #1

[Date]

«AddressBlock»

«GreetingLine»

Hi, my name is [*AGENT'S NAME*], with [*COMPANY NAME*], and I just sold the home at [*LISTING ADDRESS*] in your neighborhood. Are you considering a move, or, would you just like to know the value of your property? Either way, call me for a FREE price evaluation on what your house might be worth on today's real estate market. I'll be glad to provide this information for you at no cost and no obligation to list.

I hope you will take the time to welcome your new neighbors to the area, and please keep my business card on file if I can help you in any way.

Yours truly,

[Agent Name]
[Agent Title]

Just Sold House In Neighborhood—Letter #2

[Date]

«AddressBlock»

«GreetingLine»

Congratulations, you have new neighbors! I'm proud to announce the sale of [*ADDRESS OF PROPERTY*] this week to [*NAME OF NEW BUYERS*]. I hope you will give the [*LAST NAME OF NEW BUYERS*] a welcome to the neighborhood.

If you have real estate needs, feel free to call me [*AGENT'S NAME*] at [*PHONE NUMBER*]. You can also visit my Web site at [Web Address] to view properties for sale and find more real estate information.

Now is a great time to buy or sell a home! For a FREE price evaluation on what your home is worth on today's real estate market, call me at [*PHONE NUMBER*].

Thanks for your time, and I hope you extend a hearty welcome to [*NAME OF NEW BUYERS*].

Yours truly,

[Agent Name]
[Agent Title]

Note: Please be sure to get permission from the buyers before sending this letter.

Short Sales

At the time of writing this text our country is facing some challenging economic situations. Many homeowners are faced with owing more monies than what their property value is worth on today's real estate market. Because of this, many lenders are utilizing what is termed a *short sale* to help struggling homeowners who were faced with this situation. Short sales can be very complicated and require a lot of legal details. The author cautions and recommends all real estate professionals to advise their clients or customers to seek a legal counsel whenever a short sale is performed.

This section of letters will help you prospect for potential business in various neighborhoods where short sales or struggling homeowners may exist. In many parts of the country you can find out when foreclosures are posted at the local courthouse. These might be good prospects for some of the letters, although it may be too late in helping these defaulting borrowers. Hopefully you will be able to assist many consumers in your area in avoiding a possible foreclosure.

Unfortunately, many people are taking advantage of homeowners who are facing these challenging situations. As real estate professionals we should strive to assist and help consumers in any way possible without charging additional fees.

Remember, short sales are challenging and time-consuming, but they can and do close on a regular basis. There are many excellent educational offerings in helping the real estate professional learn and understand more about short sales, and it is highly advised that you investigate this more to help with selling short sales in your marketplace.

Finally, there are options for consumers who are facing trying times. Being there, listening and helping where you can, will be a help many people will remember for the rest of their lives.

Short-Sale Letters

[Date]

«AddressBlock»

«GreetingLine»

Hello, my name is (*AGENT NAME*), a real estate sales associate with (*COMPANY NAME*) in (*CITY*). Due to the current economic conditions, many homeowners have faced severe hardships in keeping up with their monthly mortgage payments. Unfortunately, a lot of hardworking people have been laid off, lost their jobs, or have had other unforeseen circumstances that have put them in severe hardship. Fortunately, many lenders are willing to work with homeowners who are in these catastrophic circumstances. As a real estate professional who works specifically in your market area and knows the ins and outs of how short sales work, I would appreciate any referrals or recommendations that you may be able to make on my behalf to anyone you might know facing a similar situation. Many people have no idea that they can be relieved from a huge financial burden. Because of this, I thought it was only appropriate in sending out letters throughout your neighborhood letting people know that there are options available if they are facing a challenging situation.

If I can answer more questions or help anyone you may know who is having a difficult time in what I have described in this letter, I would love to help them overcome this obstacle. There are options available, and I may have some solutions. I have enclosed my business card with my contact information if I can assist.

I appreciate your time, and I also appreciate and thank you in advance for telling others about me.

Yours truly,

[Agent Name]
[Agent Title]

Short-Sale Letters

[Date]

«AddressBlock»

«GreetingLine»

Hello, my name is (*AGENT NAME*), a real estate sales associate with (*COMPANY NAME*) in (*CITY*). Unfortunately, we have seen some of the highest foreclosure numbers in our country's history over the last few months. These are hardworking people who have always paid their bills on time and who are facing unknown territories in their lives. The sad reality is that most of the people who have fallen into foreclosure had other options available to them. Today, many lenders will do what is commonly referred to as a *short sale* or help with a re-modification of an existing home loan. I would love to assist anyone you may know who is facing a hardship or challenge as described in this letter. Thankfully, there are options and I am willing to help and provide possible solutions to your friends. There is no fee for me to help in these particular areas unless of course they would need my assistance in marketing their home and selling their property through a short sale. These questions and many others could be answered during our initial consultation.

I appreciate your time and thank you in advance for referring my name to anyone you may know in your neighborhood or at work facing a challenging or threatening situation—of the possibility of losing their home.

Yours truly,

[Agent Name]
[Agent Title]

Short-Sale Letters

[Date]

«AddressBlock»

«GreetingLine»

Hello, my name is (*AGENT NAME*), a real estate sales associate working with (*COMPANY NAME*) in (*CITY*). It seems that there is not a day that goes by where foreclosures and the negative real estate industry are played out in the news media. Record-high foreclosures, bankruptcies, loss of jobs, layoffs, and the list can go on and on. I am not a gloom and doom person, and I definitely don't want you to think that there is no activity going on in the real estate market, because we are seeing movement and an increased activity among buyers in our marketplace.

What I do want to point out is that many sellers feel as though they are forced out of the home selling market because what they owe on their home is more than the current market value of their property. True, this can be a huge obstacle for sellers to overcome; however, many lenders are willing to work through either a loan re-modification and/or a short sale to get around these issues.

A short sale is basically where the lender is willing to accept a lesser amount in exchange for a full payoff of your loan. There are many legal and financial requirements that must be met before this can take place, but it is an option for some sellers. I in no way hold all of the answers to these specific questions; however, I would be glad to visit with you or your friends through an initial consultation to determine if a short sale is a possibility. If I feel that there is a preliminary chance that a short sale may be a possibility and you have a desire to sell your property, our next step would be to put you in touch with the correct legal experts who can handle the specific legality questions that you may have. What I wanted you to be aware of is that there are options and solutions that we can work through to help you get your home sold, even though you may owe more than what it is currently worth.

If you would like to visit me more, please feel free to call me at (*AGENT PHONE NUMBER*) or e-mail me at (*AGENT E-MAIL*). I appreciate your time and look forward to hearing from you soon.

Yours truly,

[Agent Name]
[Agent Title]

Short-Sale Letters

[Date]

«AddressBlock»

«GreetingLine»

Could a short sale be right for you? Today, many homeowners are faced with a mortgage loan balance that is in excess of what their current property value is worth in today's current real estate market. Unfortunately, many sellers feel there is nothing they can do in this situation. Many homeowners are allowing their homes to go back to the lender and opting for a foreclosure that will now negatively impact their credit report for many years.

Thankfully, there are several options and solutions with many lenders today. A short sale is a complicated process, but is one method I am familiar with and would like to discuss with you in greater detail if you have an interest.

My direct line is (*AGENT PHONE NUMBER*) and my e-mail address is (*AGENT E-MAIL*).

Don't just settle for a foreclosure and let your property go back to the bank. Explore all of the options and opportunities that may be available to you. Call or write me today so we can begin the process to determine what solution will work best for you.

Yours truly,

[Agent Name]
[Agent Title]

Short-Sale Letters— Requesting Permission For Information From Lender

Loan # _____

Borrower(s) Name(s): _____

Legal Description: _____

Property Address _____

City _____ State _____ Zip Code _____

We give our permission for you to discuss our loan details to our real estate

agent, _____ .

Signed— _____   _____

      Borrower   Date

_____   _____

      Borrower   Date

[Date]

«AddressBlock»

«GreetingLine»

As per your request, here is the information that you asked for regarding the possibility of doing a short sale at (*ADDRESS OF PROPERTY*).

If there is any additional information that I can provide for you, please do not hesitate to give me a call. I sincerely appreciate your company considering this short sale for (*BORROWER'S NAME*). These are good people, caught up in an unforeseen situation that has put them in the difficult position of requesting a short sale.

Again, thank you for your time, and I look forward to hearing from you soon.

Yours truly,

[Agent Name]
[Agent Title]

Short-Sale Letters—Thank You For Helping With Short Sale To Lender

[Date]

«AddressBlock»

«GreetingLine»

Thank you for working so promptly and quickly on getting us an approval for (*BORROWER'S NAME*). Allowing my clients this option of conducting a short sale on their property is a huge weight and burden lifted off of their shoulders. Your quick and professional attention in getting this approved is greatly appreciated.

Thank you so much!

Yours truly,

[Agent Name]
[Agent Title]

Short-Sale Letters— Requesting If Short Sale Is Possible

[Date]

«AddressBlock»

«GreetingLine»

This e-mail is to request the possibility of doing a short sale for (*BORROWER'S NAME, LOAN NUMBER, ADDRESS OF PROPERTY*). (*BORROWER'S NAME*) have had some very trying circumstances over the past few years and unfortunately with the downturn of our economy there is no way they can sell their home on today's real estate market to pay off all of their obligations and debts with your company.

As their real estate agent, I am asking to find out if a short sale is a possibility with your company? If so, could you please provide me with the requirements or Web site where I can get the information to begin applying for this process for them?

Thank you for your time, and I look forward to hearing from you soon.

Yours truly,

[Agent Name]
[Agent Title]

Short-Sale Letters— To Buyer's Purchasing A Short-Sale Home

[Date]

«AddressBlock»

«GreetingLine»

Thank you again for allowing me the opportunity to write the sales contract on (*ADDRESS OF PROPERTY*). As I indicated to you during the time of writing the offer to purchase, this accepted sales contract is contingent upon the seller's lender agreeing to your agreed-upon sales price and an approved short sale. Please remember, that short-sale transactions move at a very slow pace and this might take some time before we have a clearance to close. In the meantime, we'll need to make sure that all of our obligations are in order so that when the seller's lender approves the short sale, we'll be ready to move forward.

If you have any questions, please do not hesitate to call me. Again, thank you for your patience and understanding of how long this process may take. Hopefully, we'll hear something soon, but if not, don't panic or get discouraged.

Yours truly,

[Agent Name]
[Agent Title]

Short-Sale Letters— To Seller's Purchasing A Short-Sale Home

[Date]

«AddressBlock»

«GreetingLine»

Thank you again for allowing me the opportunity to write the sales contract on (*ADDRESS OF PROPERTY*). As I indicated to you during the time of presenting the offer to purchase, this accepted sales contract is contingent upon your lender agreeing to your agreed-upon sales price and an approved short sale. Please remember, that short-sale transactions move at a very slow pace and this might take some time before we have a clearance to close.

If you have any questions, please do not hesitate to call me. Again, thank you for your patience and understanding of how long this process may take. Hopefully, we'll hear something back from your lender soon, but if not, don't panic or get discouraged.

Yours truly,

[Agent Name]
[Agent Title]

Short-Sale Letters— Follow-Up For Seller After Contract Letter #2

[Date]

«AddressBlock»

«GreetingLine»

Just a quick note to let you know that I have sent all of the necessary paperwork in to (*BORROWER'S LENDER*) with regards to doing a possible short sale on your property. Please note that these types of transactions move very slowly and sometimes it can be several days before we hear back from anyone at the lending institution. I promise that as soon as I hear something I will be in touch with you and update you with the status. In the meantime, always feel free to call me if you have any questions or concerns.

As always, I appreciate the opportunity to be of service to you with your real estate needs. I'm hopeful and optimistic that we will be able to move forward with a short sale on your property soon.

Yours truly,

[Agent Name]
[Agent Title]

Sphere of Influence

O ne of the most essential marketing suggestions I give to my students as I teach real estate courses around the United States and abroad is to follow up with your *sphere of influence*! Some real estate professionals refer to this as their *center of influence*. Whatever you refer to this group as, personal friends, bird dogs, etc., this group of acquaintances that you know and can go to for referrals is golden.

For years the National Association of REALTORS® has asked buyers and sellers how they chose a real estate agent for their closed transaction. One of the top responses has always been, *"from the recommendation or referral from a friend, co-worker or family member."* As this research indicates, staying in touch with your sphere of influence is a vital key to your success as a real estate professional. Let's admit, most everyone feels comfortable working with someone who has been recommended to them by a close friend, and the only way you can get people to recommend you as a real estate agent is to provide good quality service along with asking your clients and customers to recommend you to their friends when they need real estate services.

It's important that you develop a good list of contacts within your sphere of influence. When I first started in real estate, my mother (my broker and my mentor) encouraged me to think about a wedding list, and who we would invite. She reminded me to put people whom I would invite to my wedding on my sphere of influence. In other words, my mother said that my wedding guests would be an excellent sphere of influence. I encourage you to think about a marriage that you might be participating in, or one that your children would be planning, and ask yourself who will you invite to the wedding? Those guests are your sphere of influence!

Another important factor about your sphere of influence is how often you contact these individuals. I believe you should contact them on a monthly basis, but it doesn't hurt to contact some of them even more frequently than monthly. Although this is a book entitled *Five Minutes to More Great Real Estate Letters*, I do encourage and suggest you use other forms of communication with your

sphere of influence. It's not a bad idea to call individuals from time to time or to stop by their house or their work just to say hello and visit with them for a quick moment. People like and appreciate a personal touch or a personal visit. Always respect your friends time, but it's okay and good to use other means of communication with your sphere of influence, and it will win big business for you in the end. Use the letters included in this book, but also remind yourself that a personal phone call, a handwritten note and an occasional visit are good ways to communicate with your group.

There is a full year of correspondence to your sphere of influence in this section. Some of the letters can also serve as e-mail messages should you so choose to correspond electronically. If you have permission to send e-mails to your sphere of influence, then you may consider using a few of these templates as e-mail message versus a printed letter, especially the market area reports.

I believe that by utilizing the letters and templates in this book, along with personal visits, phone calls and other forms of communication, your sphere of influence will provide you with referrals for many years into the future.

Twelve-Month Sphere of Influence Campaign: January

[Date]

«AddressBlock»

«GreetingLine»

Why January Is a Great Time to Sell Your Home.

Many people believe January is not a good time to sell real estate. On the contrary, January can actually be an excellent time to place your property for sale in your local real estate market. Why would January be such a good time to sell? It's the simple economic principle of supply and demand. Generally, most people want to wait until springtime to sell their property, when, in fact, there are still many people (buyers) in the market looking for available homes. Therefore, since there is a limited supply of homes for sale, but still an adequate number of buyers available, your property will have a greater opportunity selling due to less competition in the marketplace.

If you have the slightest inclination about selling your property and you've told yourself that it may be better to wait a month or two before putting it out on the market, please think again. January can be an excellent time to get your property sold at a competitive price.

If you would like to visit with me regarding current information on what your house may be worth in today's real estate market, please call me at [*Agent Phone Number*] or e-mail me [*Agent E-Mail*]. As always, I appreciate your friendship and your business and want you to know that I'm always here for your real estate needs.

Yours truly,

[Agent Name]
[Agent Title]

February

[Date]

«AddressBlock»

«GreetingLine»

Can you believe that spring is only one month away? It's always amazing to me how quickly the winter months can fly by. It's exciting that spring is just around the corner, and with the entering of this new season, our real estate market typically begins to push into high gear.

Many of my friends are contemplating a new move or a possible move as the home buying and selling season approaches; therefore, I wanted to prepare a short [*Report, Link To YouTube, Podcast, Etc.*] on what happened in the [*Insert Previous Year's*] real estate market. This information is compiled from our local Multiple Listing Service [*Or Other Source for Your Area*] and gives you a good snapshot of what the average sales price of homes have sold for along with other information that you might find useful.

If you're thinking about buying or selling real estate in the coming months or know of someone who may be in the market to buy or sell, please keep me in mind. I would love to work with you, and I always appreciate your referrals.

As always, thank you for your business and your friendship, and I appreciate you supporting me in my real estate endeavors.

Yours truly,

[Agent Name]
[Agent Title]

March

[Date]

«AddressBlock»

«GreetingLine»

I Need Your Help!

March is normally the beginning of home buying and selling season in [*City*]. The month typically starts out with our listing inventory growing and building at a rapid rate. Many new sellers enter the marketplace and one of the key ingredients for any real estate professional is to have and maintain an adequate listing supply. I realize that you may not necessarily be in the market to sell your real estate; however, you may know of someone who has indicated that they are thinking about selling their property. According to the National Association of REALTORS®, a large percentage of people choose a real estate professional based on a friend's, family member's or coworker's recommendation. Because of this fact, I'm asking that as you hear about individuals or families who are thinking about buying or selling real estate, do refer my name for possible business.

As a real estate professional, referrals from friends like you play a vital role in my daily business. I've enclosed a few business cards for you to distribute to anyone you may hear about, who is thinking about selling or buying their home.

I thank you in advance for your help on this request. As always, I appreciate your business and your friendship, and I look forward to serving you and your friends with their real estate needs in the future.

Yours truly,

[Agent Name]
[Agent Title]

April

[Date]

«AddressBlock»

«GreetingLine»

You may have already filed your taxes, or perhaps you're in the process of getting your information together. My good friend [*Insert Tax Advisor's Name and Company Name*] has provided me with this [*Insert Booklet Or Free Report*] to help you in getting your tax information together for this filing season. This has been a great help for me and I hope you enjoy it as well.

Keep me in mind if you have any real estate listing needs in the future. And don't forget, I always love referrals from my friends and clients. They're a vital part of my business!

Yours truly,

[Agent Name]
[Agent Title]

This letter you might work in conjunction with a local CPA in your marketplace. You may need to obtain some booklets from your local CPA or tax advisor. You might also consider doing this as an optional January or February letter.

April—#2

[Date]

«AddressBlock»

«GreetingLine»

It's time to cut the grass again, along with many other exterior home improvement projects. Oftentimes these small maintenance items can have a major impact on your property's value. I have included in the following list a few things that you may consider putting on your to-do list, which will help maintain and improve your property's value. I realize that not everyone on my monthly mailing list is a homeowner, but the information provided is always good knowledge for both buyers and sellers. As a future homeowner, following this suggested list regularly can help you achieve the maximum amount of money possible when you are ready to sell.

- Consider painting the exterior, any trim, soffits and especially the front door
- Install fresh mulch or rock in flower beds and other existing covered areas
- If your house does not need painting, consider renting an exterior high-pressure washing machine
- Repair or replace any torn screens or broken windows
- Caulk and seal cracks in sidewalks or driveway
- Trim any shrubs or bushes that may have grown
- Apply a good fertilizer to help maintain a lush, green lawn, and prohibit weed growth
- Clean gutters and make sure all down-spouts have splash blocks, or make sure water is diverted away from existing housing foundation
- Consider planting flowers in strategic locations that will provide color throughout the year

You might also consider driving around your neighborhood to get ideas about what others are doing to improve the exterior appearance of their home, and follow through with some of the same ideas.

Some of these suggestions will require a small amount of funds to repair; however, in the long run, they will help aid to the increased property value of your home's net worth.

Neglecting to maintain or follow the suggestions on this list can become a major price discount in potential buyers' eyes if you go to put your home on the market. By doing a little bit in maintaining these areas each year, you will witness an enormous return on your investment in time and money.

As always, thanks for your support and business. Remember that I love referrals you send me of others who are thinking about buying or selling real estate. Let me know if I can help you in the future as well

Yours truly,

[Agent Name]
[Agent Title]

May

[Date]

«AddressBlock»

«GreetingLine»

Now that the first three months are complete and we've had time during the month of April to compile all the sales data for the first quarter of [*Year*], I wanted to share with you my [*Area Name*] market report. I believe you'll find some interesting information in this report about what's going on in our local marketplace regarding the real estate industry.

Remember to tell your friends, family members, and coworkers about me if they're in the market to buy or sell real estate, or if they would like a copy of this report. And of course, I would love to help you when you're ready to buy or sell your next home.

As always, thank you for your friendship and your business, and let me know if I can help.

Yours truly,

[Agent Name]
[Agent Title]

June

[Date]

«AddressBlock»

«GreetingLine»

Now that school's out of session, kids are home for the season, vacations are being planned, and summer activities are under way, it's a good time to remind you to put family and friends first. Remember that life is short! I would encourage you to sit down and plan some of those activities and trips you've been thinking about but have put off because of other plans or work. Make this summer one to remember and one that you'll cherish for years to come.

Enjoy the days ahead, and I'd love to hear about your completed and fulfilled adventures.

Yours truly,

[Agent Name]
[Agent Title]

July

[Date]

«AddressBlock»

«GreetingLine»

As we celebrate another year of our nation's beginning, I wanted to write and remind you that along with all the heritage and rich blessings around our country's founding is our right for homeownership. We are fortunate that we have the ability to buy and sell real estate in a country such as ours.

As you take time to reflect on our nation's birthday and all of those who have fought so hard for our freedom throughout history, let's remember how our founding fathers allowed us an opportunity for homeownership.

As a real estate professional, I'm reminded and appreciative of this privilege and I'm always eager to help others in the home buying and selling process. Let me know if I can help, and please keep me in mind for any referrals you may hear about when someone wants to buy or sell real estate.

As always I appreciate your friendship, thank you for your support, and let me know if I can help you.

Yours truly,

[Agent Name]
[Agent Title]

August

[Date]

«AddressBlock»

«GreetingLine»

It's Almost School Time …

As vacations wind down and everyone prepares for school, real estate continues to play an integral role in many families' lives during the month of August. It's actually a win-win situation for both buyers and sellers. True, there is a lot on everyone's mind and the home buying process can slow down a bit, so if you're a purchaser it may be a great time to negotiate on your next home.

For a seller, many of your competitive listings are going off the market after a six-month period, so your competition is greatly reduced. Therefore, those buyers who are out in the marketplace may not have as many choices to choose from, and keeping your listing or putting your listing on the market may, in fact, be a good decision.

Real estate has been and always will be an excellent investment for you, so regardless of whether you're a buyer or a seller, it's always a good time to buy or sell real estate!

Let me know if I can help you in any way regarding the purchase or the sale of your next home. I hope you had a great summer, and I look forward to hearing from you soon.

Yours truly,

[Agent Name]
[Agent Title]

PS: *Don't forget I love referrals, and it's a vital part of my business. Any time you hear of someone who wants to buy or sell real estate I would appreciate you letting them know about my services and giving me a good recommendation. Thanks!*

September

[Date]

«AddressBlock»

«GreetingLine»

Now that the first half of the real estate year is booked complete and the numbers have been finalized, I wanted to share with you my mid-term housing report for [*City*]. This report contains all the sales data for the first half of this calendar year. I believe you'll find some interesting information in this report about what's going on in our local marketplace regarding the real estate industry.

Remember to tell your friends, family members, and coworkers about me if they're in the market to buy or sell real estate, or if they would like a copy of this report. And of course, I would love to help you when you're ready to buy or sell your next home.

As always, thank you for your friendship and your business, and let me know if I can help.

Yours truly,

[Agent Name]
[Agent Title]

October

[Date]

«AddressBlock»

«GreetingLine»

I'm often asked why some homes sell and others don't. I've put together ten reasons why homes normally do not sell. This enclosed report is good information/ knowledge for anyone who owns a home or may be thinking about purchasing a home in the near future. Regardless of whether you currently own a home or not, many people are faced with selling a home at some point during the course of their lifetime, and understanding and knowing this information can be a big help for you as a homeowner.

Don't forget I love referrals, and it's a vital part of my business. Any time you hear of someone who wants to buy or sell real estate I would appreciate you letting them know about my services and giving me a good recommendation. Thanks for your friendship!

Yours truly,

[Agent Name]
[Agent Title]

You can obtain this free report from my book Five Minutes to Great Real Estate Marketing Ideas *along with many other free reports, letters, and marketing ideas to help grow your real estate career. As my appreciation to you for purchasing this book, I would love to send you this free report; please go to www.RealEstateTechGuy.com, click on the tab "resources" and click on the link "five minute customers," to request your FREE copy.*

November

[Date]

«AddressBlock»

«GreetingLine»

I wanted to write you a short letter and tell you how thankful I am for your friendship and your support in my real estate career. Without friends like you telling others about my real estate services, I would not be where I'm at today. You play an important role in my success, and I wanted to share with you my appreciation and my thankfulness in all you do.

I hope you have a wonderful Thanksgiving, and remember you can always count on me for real estate advice or help.

Enjoy your holidays and let me know if I can help anyway.

Yours truly,

[Agent Name]
[Agent Title]

December

[Date]

«AddressBlock»

«GreetingLine»

Did you know that winter is often an excellent time to sell real estate? Generally there is still a good supply of buyers looking for real estate but a smaller number of properties to choose from, which leads to what we term a "seller's market." A seller's market is probably the best time for you to sell your home. Unfortunately, many sellers take their real estate off the market until springtime, thinking they can get top dollar next year. True, spring is an excellent time to list real estate, but the competition is much greater, allowing buyers more to choose from. In reality, it's generally a better time to sell and get more money during the winter months when the competition is less.

If you know of someone considering a move soon, please remind that person of my services. The success of my career is dependent on referrals from friends like you, and despite what many people may claim, now is a great time to buy or sell real estate!

I appreciate your time *[Letter Name]*, and thanks in advance for always remembering me when you think of real estate.

Yours truly,

[Agent Name]
[Agent Title]

Letters to Buyers

For the buyer's section of *Five Minutes to More Great Real Estate Letters*, I have taken the approach that most real estate agents will be sending a greater quantity of e-mails versus general real estate letters through the U.S. Postal system. As noted earlier in the text, most of the documents in this book are designed to function as either a letter or an e-mail message. However, many buyer leads come in through the Internet today from an agent or company Web site, and a good drip marketing campaign is essential to capture these leads over the long haul.

An interesting statistic that I heard at a recent real estate conference discussed the typical home buyer and Internet relationships. At this conference, the speaker noted that most home buyers will spend anywhere from eight to ten weeks looking for homes online. They will also visit five company Web sites and complete (on average three different) inquiry forms on those company Web sites. The surprising statistic to me is that only 48% of the buyers who completed the inquiry forms heard back from a real estate agent! For the other 52%, who did receive a reply, it was over 24 hours before they heard back from the agent or company.

There are a couple of interesting points to note about the statistics: First, if buyers are spending eight to ten weeks online looking for homes, and they inquire about properties with the various real estate agencies, shouldn't you have a good drip marketing campaign in place to follow up with these buyers regularly? With so many buyers never hearing from anyone, it only makes good sense to have a good drip marketing campaign where you can follow up with these potential prospects. Unfortunately, many real estate agents do not like the Internet leads because they feel they go absolutely nowhere, when, in reality, an Internet buyer lead is a good prospect. You must consistently stay in touch and follow up to win business with the Internet buyer.

Included with *Five Minutes to More Great Real Estate Letters* are two eight-week plan of actions (drip marketing campaigns), along with other ideas you can share with buyers who may visit your Web site and register to receive more information. If you want to convert the business from buyers, you must incorporate a good drip marketing campaign with e-mail messages that go out on a consistent basis.

Eight-Week Drip Marketing Campaign to Buyers

Campaign #1
E-Mail Message #1

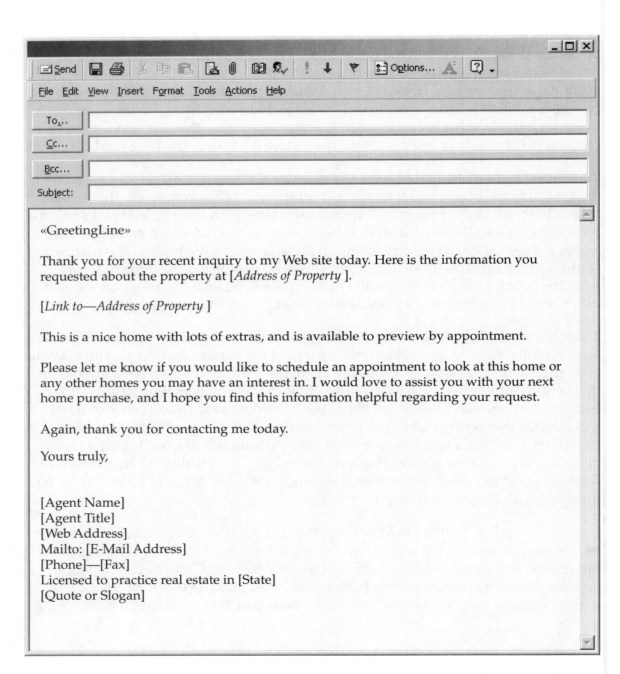

«GreetingLine»

Thank you for your recent inquiry to my Web site today. Here is the information you requested about the property at [*Address of Property*].

[*Link to—Address of Property*]

This is a nice home with lots of extras, and is available to preview by appointment.

Please let me know if you would like to schedule an appointment to look at this home or any other homes you may have an interest in. I would love to assist you with your next home purchase, and I hope you find this information helpful regarding your request.

Again, thank you for contacting me today.

Yours truly,

[Agent Name]
[Agent Title]
[Web Address]
Mailto: [E-Mail Address]
[Phone]—[Fax]
Licensed to practice real estate in [State]
[Quote or Slogan]

Eight-Week Drip Marketing Campaign to Buyers

E-Mail Message #2

Send | File Edit View Insert Format Tools Actions Help

To...

Cc...

Bcc...

Subject:

«GreetingLine»

I wanted to follow up with you about the information I recently sent you regarding the property at [*Address of Property*], and ask if there are any additional questions I could answer for you about this property.

I understand that this home may not meet all the criteria you would love to have in your new home. Therefore, I wanted to tell you about an interesting feature our Multiple Listings Service offers for potential buyers like you. It's a "customized" home search, which allows me the opportunity to input the features you want or desire in your next home, which in turn will notify you and me of new listings that become available. It's kind of like you becoming the first person to hear about the new listings that match your desired dream home when they enter the real estate marketplace.

I would be happy to set up a customized search for you. Of course there is no charge to do this for you, and it will only take me a few minutes to put in place. The most effective way to set this up is for you to call me at your earliest convenience. You may contact me at, [*Address of Property*], or you may also e-mail me with a list of your wants and needs for your next home at [*Agent E-Mail*].

Again, I appreciate your recent e-mail, and please do not hesitate to contact me if this customized home search is something you have an interest in.

Yours truly,

[Agent Name]
[Agent Title]
[Web Address]
Mailto: [E-Mail Address]
[Phone]—[Fax]
Licensed to practice real estate in [State]
[Quote or Slogan]

Eight-Week Drip Marketing Campaign to Buyers

E-Mail Message #3

«GreetingLine»

The home buying process can be a challenging process, and I realize many home buyers prefer to use the Internet to search for homes prior to contacting a real estate agent to begin physically looking at homes. I commend you for taking these first steps, and you are taking the right action by narrowing your choices down to a location and price range before you begin to look at homes in person.

Please know that I would love to help you with your next home purchase, and I can assist you in several areas of the sale, working with you as a "buyer's agent." If you would like to find out more about how I can represent you in the real estate transaction, please contact me at [*Agent Phone Number*], I would be happy to visit with you.

Thanks again for visiting my Web site recently, and please know I am here to help you answer any of your real estate questions.

Yours truly,

[Agent Name]
[Agent Title]
[Web Address]
Mailto: [E-Mail Address]
[Phone]—[Fax]
Licensed to practice real estate in [State]
[Quote or Slogan]

Eight-Week Drip Marketing Campaign to Buyers

E-Mail Message #4

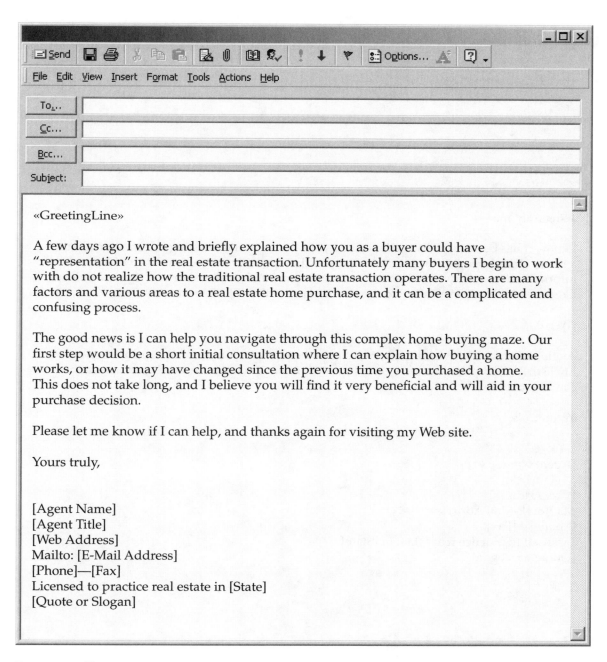

«GreetingLine»

A few days ago I wrote and briefly explained how you as a buyer could have "representation" in the real estate transaction. Unfortunately many buyers I begin to work with do not realize how the traditional real estate transaction operates. There are many factors and various areas to a real estate home purchase, and it can be a complicated and confusing process.

The good news is I can help you navigate through this complex home buying maze. Our first step would be a short initial consultation where I can explain how buying a home works, or how it may have changed since the previous time you purchased a home. This does not take long, and I believe you will find it very beneficial and will aid in your purchase decision.

Please let me know if I can help, and thanks again for visiting my Web site.

Yours truly,

[Agent Name]
[Agent Title]
[Web Address]
Mailto: [E-Mail Address]
[Phone]—[Fax]
Licensed to practice real estate in [State]
[Quote or Slogan]

Eight-Week Drip Marketing Campaign to Buyers

E-Mail Message #5

Send | File Edit View Insert Format Tools Actions Help

To...

Cc...

Bcc...

Subject:

«GreetingLine»

I know it has been awhile since I received your first e-mail requesting information about a home I listed, but I did want to remind you that my Web site contains a lot of helpful information about buying a home. I've included my Web address for you if you would like to return to my Web site and check out many of the "FREE" resources.

[*Web Address*]

Again, thank you for visiting my Web site in the past and for your inquiry about one of my listings, and please feel free to call or write me if you have any additional questions I can assist you with.

Yours truly,

[Agent Name]
[Agent Title]
[Web Address]
Mailto: [E-Mail Address]
[Phone]—[Fax]
Licensed to practice real estate in [State]
[Quote or Slogan]

Eight-Week Drip Marketing Campaign to Buyers

E-Mail Message #6

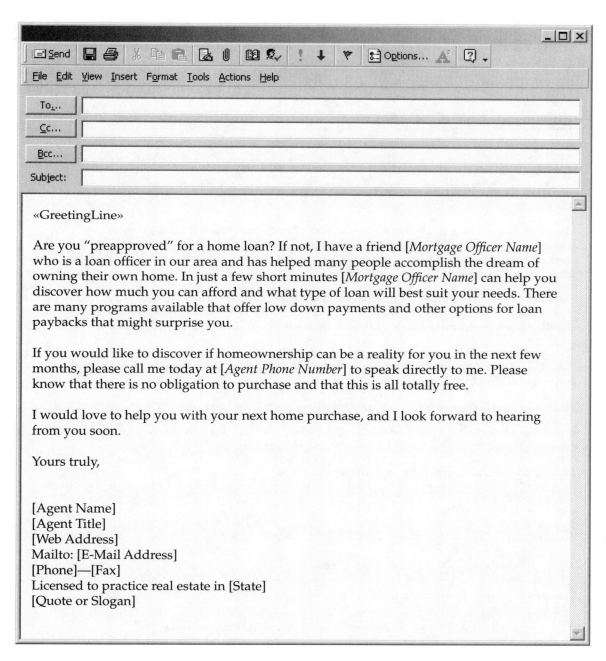

«GreetingLine»

Are you "preapproved" for a home loan? If not, I have a friend [*Mortgage Officer Name*] who is a loan officer in our area and has helped many people accomplish the dream of owning their own home. In just a few short minutes [*Mortgage Officer Name*] can help you discover how much you can afford and what type of loan will best suit your needs. There are many programs available that offer low down payments and other options for loan paybacks that might surprise you.

If you would like to discover if homeownership can be a reality for you in the next few months, please call me today at [*Agent Phone Number*] to speak directly to me. Please know that there is no obligation to purchase and that this is all totally free.

I would love to help you with your next home purchase, and I look forward to hearing from you soon.

Yours truly,

[Agent Name]
[Agent Title]
[Web Address]
Mailto: [E-Mail Address]
[Phone]—[Fax]
Licensed to practice real estate in [State]
[Quote or Slogan]

Eight-Week Drip Marketing Campaign to Buyers

E-Mail Message #7

«GreetingLine»

Many buyers are taking advantage of the low interest rates and attractive home prices by subscribing to my monthly newsletter. My newsletter contains tips for buying a home, as well as some of the best buys in our marketplace. I'd love to add you to my e-newsletter list, it's free, and I think you will find a wealth of information each month.

Each month you will receive new tips like this one: *"How buyers are taking advantage of the HUD 203 (K) home loans on some of the foreclosed properties that need many improvements. The HUD 203 (K) loan will allow you to borrow extra money to help make the repairs on these discounted foreclosed homes."*

To sign up for my FREE e-newsletter designed especially for buyers, send an e-mail to [*Agent E-Mail*]. I'll be sure to add you to my list, and, don't worry, I never share or sell any of my names and e-mail addresses to anyone.

Become an informed buyer before you enter the marketplace, subscribe to my FREE e-newsletter today.

If you're ready to find out just how much home you will qualify for and ready to get preapproved, call me at [*Agent Phone Number*] to schedule your appointment today.

I appreciate your time, and I hope to hear from you soon.

Yours truly,

[Agent Name]
[Agent Title]
[Web Address]
Mailto: [E-Mail Address]
[Phone]—[Fax]
Licensed to practice real estate in [State]
[Quote or Slogan]

Note, this letter is also found in the "Prospecting Section—Apartments."

Eight-Week Drip Marketing Campaign to Buyers

E-Mail Message #8

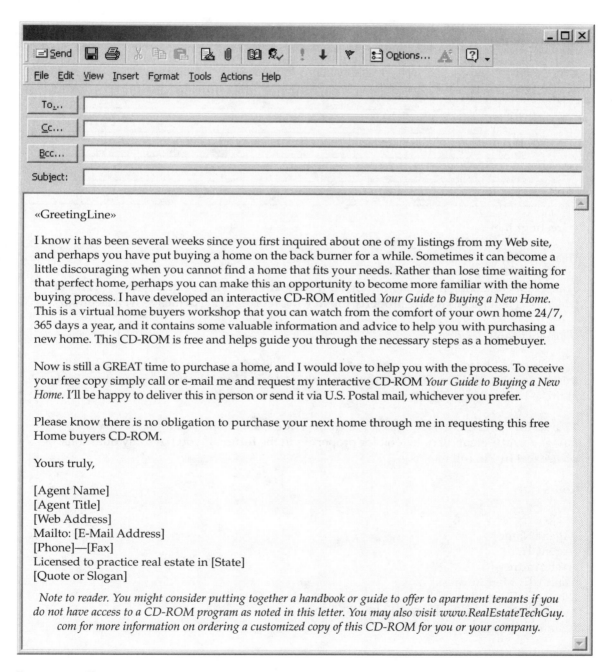

«GreetingLine»

I know it has been several weeks since you first inquired about one of my listings from my Web site, and perhaps you have put buying a home on the back burner for a while. Sometimes it can become a little discouraging when you cannot find a home that fits your needs. Rather than lose time waiting for that perfect home, perhaps you can make this an opportunity to become more familiar with the home buying process. I have developed an interactive CD-ROM entitled *Your Guide to Buying a New Home.* This is a virtual home buyers workshop that you can watch from the comfort of your own home 24/7, 365 days a year, and it contains some valuable information and advice to help you with purchasing a new home. This CD-ROM is free and helps guide you through the necessary steps as a homebuyer.

Now is still a GREAT time to purchase a home, and I would love to help you with the process. To receive your free copy simply call or e-mail me and request my interactive CD-ROM *Your Guide to Buying a New Home.* I'll be happy to deliver this in person or send it via U.S. Postal mail, whichever you prefer.

Please know there is no obligation to purchase your next home through me in requesting this free Home buyers CD-ROM.

Yours truly,

[Agent Name]
[Agent Title]
[Web Address]
Mailto: [E-Mail Address]
[Phone]—[Fax]
Licensed to practice real estate in [State]
[Quote or Slogan]

Note to reader. You might consider putting together a handbook or guide to offer to apartment tenants if you do not have access to a CD-ROM program as noted in this letter. You may also visit www.RealEstateTechGuy. com for more information on ordering a customized copy of this CD-ROM for you or your company.

Eight-Week Drip Marketing Campaign to Buyers

Campaign #2
E-Mail Message #1

Send | File Edit View Insert Format Tools Actions Help

To...

Cc...

Bcc...

Subject:

«GreetingLine»

Dear BUYER,

Thanks for contacting me today through our company Web site regarding the property at [*Address*]. Here's a link to the property for viewing more specific details as well as photos.

[*Link to Listing*]

If you would like to make an appointment to preview this property, I'd be happy to set this up for you. You can reach me at this number [*Agent Phone Number*] or e-mail me back at this e-mail address [*Agent E-Mail*].

Thanks for visiting our Web site on the World Wide Web. I hope you found it easy to navigate and a great place to look for properties in the future. If you have any questions, please feel free to call me.

Yours truly,

[Agent Name]
[Agent Title]
[Web Address]
Mailto: [E-Mail Address]
[Phone]—[Fax]
Licensed to practice real estate in [State]
[Quote or Slogan]

Eight-Week Drip Marketing Campaign to Buyers

Campaign #2
E-Mail Message #2

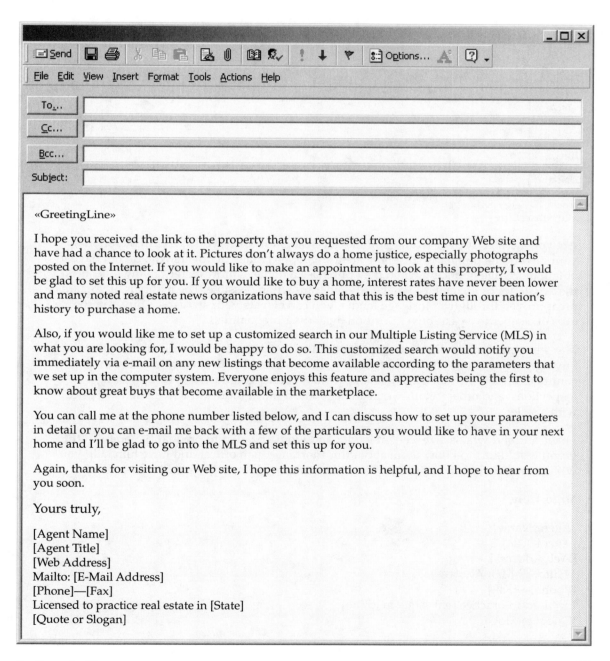

«GreetingLine»

I hope you received the link to the property that you requested from our company Web site and have had a chance to look at it. Pictures don't always do a home justice, especially photographs posted on the Internet. If you would like to make an appointment to look at this property, I would be glad to set this up for you. If you would like to buy a home, interest rates have never been lower and many noted real estate news organizations have said that this is the best time in our nation's history to purchase a home.

Also, if you would like me to set up a customized search in our Multiple Listing Service (MLS) in what you are looking for, I would be happy to do so. This customized search would notify you immediately via e-mail on any new listings that become available according to the parameters that we set up in the computer system. Everyone enjoys this feature and appreciates being the first to know about great buys that become available in the marketplace.

You can call me at the phone number listed below, and I can discuss how to set up your parameters in detail or you can e-mail me back with a few of the particulars you would like to have in your next home and I'll be glad to go into the MLS and set this up for you.

Again, thanks for visiting our Web site, I hope this information is helpful, and I hope to hear from you soon.

Yours truly,

[Agent Name]
[Agent Title]
[Web Address]
Mailto: [E-Mail Address]
[Phone]—[Fax]
Licensed to practice real estate in [State]
[Quote or Slogan]

Eight-Week Drip Marketing Campaign to Buyers

Campaign #2
E-Mail Message #3

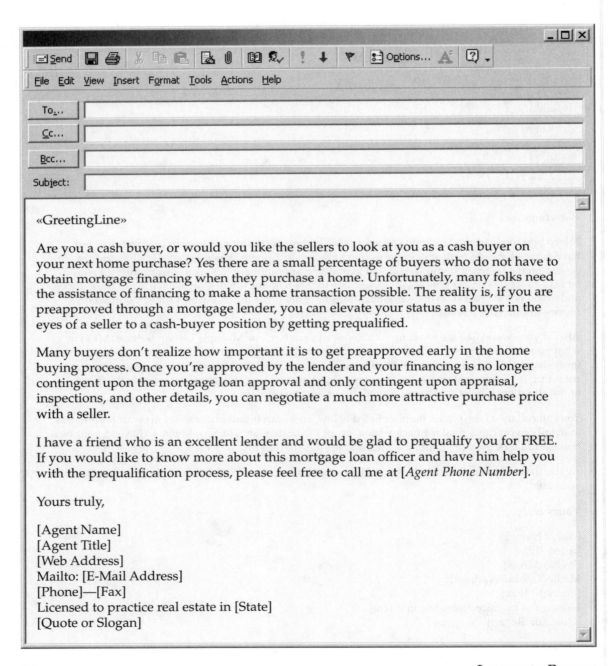

«GreetingLine»

Are you a cash buyer, or would you like the sellers to look at you as a cash buyer on your next home purchase? Yes there are a small percentage of buyers who do not have to obtain mortgage financing when they purchase a home. Unfortunately, many folks need the assistance of financing to make a home transaction possible. The reality is, if you are preapproved through a mortgage lender, you can elevate your status as a buyer in the eyes of a seller to a cash-buyer position by getting prequalified.

Many buyers don't realize how important it is to get preapproved early in the home buying process. Once you're approved by the lender and your financing is no longer contingent upon the mortgage loan approval and only contingent upon appraisal, inspections, and other details, you can negotiate a much more attractive purchase price with a seller.

I have a friend who is an excellent lender and would be glad to prequalify you for FREE. If you would like to know more about this mortgage loan officer and have him help you with the prequalification process, please feel free to call me at [*Agent Phone Number*].

Yours truly,

[Agent Name]
[Agent Title]
[Web Address]
Mailto: [E-Mail Address]
[Phone]—[Fax]
Licensed to practice real estate in [State]
[Quote or Slogan]

Eight-Week Drip Marketing Campaign to Buyers

Campaign #2
E-Mail Message #4

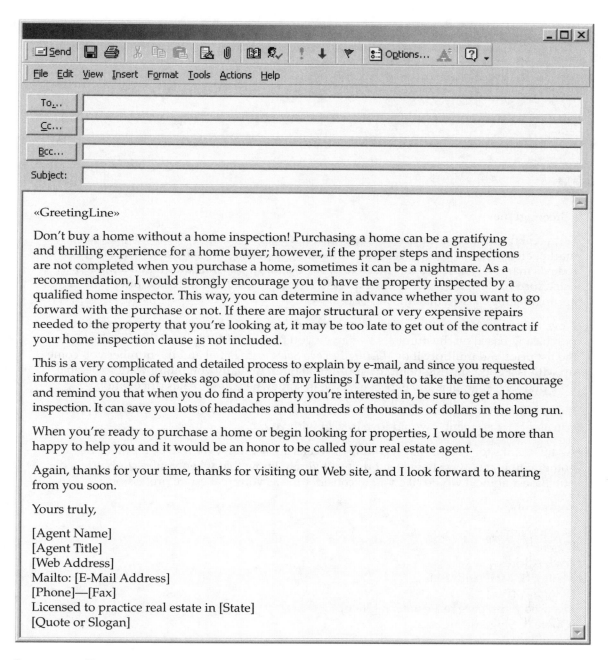

«GreetingLine»

Don't buy a home without a home inspection! Purchasing a home can be a gratifying and thrilling experience for a home buyer; however, if the proper steps and inspections are not completed when you purchase a home, sometimes it can be a nightmare. As a recommendation, I would strongly encourage you to have the property inspected by a qualified home inspector. This way, you can determine in advance whether you want to go forward with the purchase or not. If there are major structural or very expensive repairs needed to the property that you're looking at, it may be too late to get out of the contract if your home inspection clause is not included.

This is a very complicated and detailed process to explain by e-mail, and since you requested information a couple of weeks ago about one of my listings I wanted to take the time to encourage and remind you that when you do find a property you're interested in, be sure to get a home inspection. It can save you lots of headaches and hundreds of thousands of dollars in the long run.

When you're ready to purchase a home or begin looking for properties, I would be more than happy to help you and it would be an honor to be called your real estate agent.

Again, thanks for your time, thanks for visiting our Web site, and I look forward to hearing from you soon.

Yours truly,

[Agent Name]
[Agent Title]
[Web Address]
Mailto: [E-Mail Address]
[Phone]—[Fax]
Licensed to practice real estate in [State]
[Quote or Slogan]

Eight-Week Drip Marketing Campaign to Buyers

Campaign #2
E-Mail Message #5

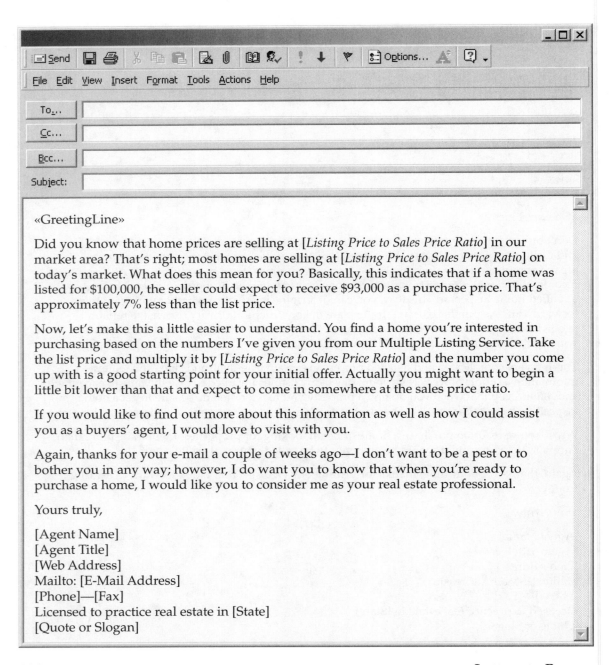

«GreetingLine»

Did you know that home prices are selling at [*Listing Price to Sales Price Ratio*] in our market area? That's right; most homes are selling at [*Listing Price to Sales Price Ratio*] on today's market. What does this mean for you? Basically, this indicates that if a home was listed for $100,000, the seller could expect to receive $93,000 as a purchase price. That's approximately 7% less than the list price.

Now, let's make this a little easier to understand. You find a home you're interested in purchasing based on the numbers I've given you from our Multiple Listing Service. Take the list price and multiply it by [*Listing Price to Sales Price Ratio*] and the number you come up with is a good starting point for your initial offer. Actually you might want to begin a little bit lower than that and expect to come in somewhere at the sales price ratio.

If you would like to find out more about this information as well as how I could assist you as a buyers' agent, I would love to visit with you.

Again, thanks for your e-mail a couple of weeks ago—I don't want to be a pest or to bother you in any way; however, I do want you to know that when you're ready to purchase a home, I would like you to consider me as your real estate professional.

Yours truly,

[Agent Name]
[Agent Title]
[Web Address]
Mailto: [E-Mail Address]
[Phone]—[Fax]
Licensed to practice real estate in [State]
[Quote or Slogan]

Eight-Week Drip Marketing Campaign to Buyers

Campaign #2
E-Mail Message #6

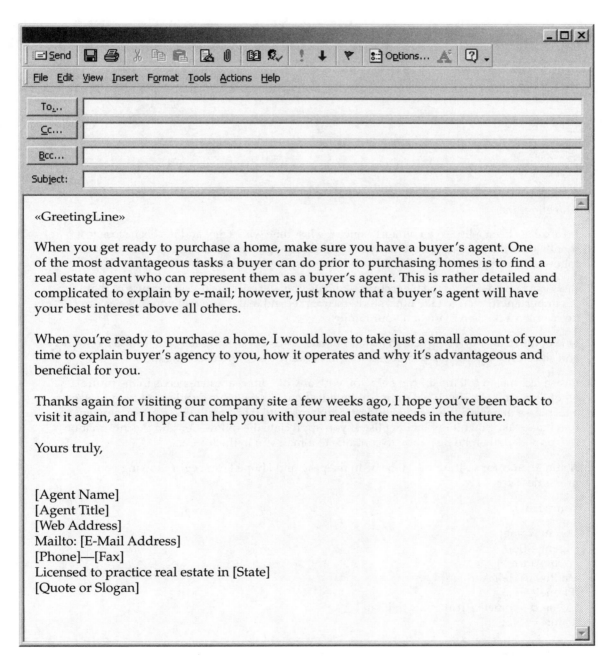

«GreetingLine»

When you get ready to purchase a home, make sure you have a buyer's agent. One of the most advantageous tasks a buyer can do prior to purchasing homes is to find a real estate agent who can represent them as a buyer's agent. This is rather detailed and complicated to explain by e-mail; however, just know that a buyer's agent will have your best interest above all others.

When you're ready to purchase a home, I would love to take just a small amount of your time to explain buyer's agency to you, how it operates and why it's advantageous and beneficial for you.

Thanks again for visiting our company site a few weeks ago, I hope you've been back to visit it again, and I hope I can help you with your real estate needs in the future.

Yours truly,

[Agent Name]
[Agent Title]
[Web Address]
Mailto: [E-Mail Address]
[Phone]—[Fax]
Licensed to practice real estate in [State]
[Quote or Slogan]

Eight-Week Drip Marketing Campaign to Buyers

Campaign #2
E-Mail Message #7

Send | File Edit View Insert Format Tools Actions Help

To...

Cc...

Bcc...

Subject:

«GreetingLine»

I realize it's been a little over a month since the last time we've met and it's been close to a month since the last time I have written to you about your real estate needs. I did want to follow up and see if you still might have an interest in purchasing a home in our area.

Buying a home is one of the biggest investments you will ever make and because of that it's important for you to take time, study the market and make sure that you make a correct decision on a home for you and your family.

One of the items I pride myself on is that I'm not a high-pressured salesperson, and I genuinely and sincerely want to help people find the right home that they're looking for.

Please feel free to call me if I can help you with any of your real estate needs in the future. I would love to help. If you have already found a home or if you've decided not to purchase one, please disregard this e-mail and just simply reply to this e-mail with a brief statement so that I may take you off my mailing list. If you appreciate the follow-ups and the information I've provided, then I'd be happy to continue to e-mail you in the future.

Again, thanks for visiting my Web site in the past, and I hope I can begin showing you properties soon.

Yours truly,

[Agent Name]
[Agent Title]
[Web Address]
Mailto: [E-Mail Address]
[Phone]—[Fax]
Licensed to practice real estate in [State]
[Quote or Slogan]

Eight-Week Drip Marketing Campaign to Buyers

Campaign #2
E-Mail Message #8

☑ Send | 🖫 🖨 | ✂ 🖺 🖻 | 🖃 📎 | 📖 🖉 | ! ↓ ▼ | 🔳 Options... 🗚 ❓ ▾

File   Edit   View   Insert   Format   Tools   Actions   Help

To...	
Cc...	
Bcc...	
Subject:	

«GreetingLine»

Several weeks ago, you inquired about a listing we had on our company's Web site. I provided you information on that property and followed up with numerous e-mails about a small part of the home buying process. Since this is my eighth e-mail to you over eight weeks, I want to first off say, please don't consider me a pest, rather a real estate professional who's eager to help you with your real estate needs. According to the National Association of REALTORS®, many home buyers will look for properties over eight to ten weeks online before they ever contact an agent to work with them. I hope that my dedication and commitment over this eight-week period has proven to you that I am the kind of real estate professional that you would chose to work with.

Through my follow-up, you have been able to determine that I am determined, dependable honest and trustworthy and ready to help. Even though you probably have not been interested in aggressively looking for properties at this moment, I hope that when you are ready to begin looking, you will consider me and my company for your real estate needs.

Again, thank you for your time. I don't mean to be a nuisance or bother you with repeated e-mails, but I do want you to know that I'm very eager in my desire to help you with your real estate needs.

Yours truly,

[Agent Name]
[Agent Title]
[Web Address]
Mailto: [E-Mail Address]
[Phone]—[Fax]
Licensed to practice real estate in [State]
[Quote or Slogan]

Campaign #2
E-Mail Message —
Bonus E-Mail Message

«GreetingLine»

Are you still interested in buying a home? Now is a GREAT time to purchase a new home, and I want you to know that if you still have the desire to purchase a home, I can help! Simply reply to this e-mail with a brief explanation as to what you would like to have in your next home, and I will begin searching for you.

If you've already purchased a home keep me in mind in the future when you get ready to sell, I'd be happy to help you in that endeavor as well.

Again, thanks for your inquiry several weeks back from my Web site. I hope that you found it helpful, and I hope you will consider working with me again in the future.

Yours truly,

[Agent Name]
[Agent Title]
[Web Address]
Mailto: [E-Mail Address]
[Phone]—[Fax]
Licensed to practice real estate in [State]
[Quote or Slogan]

Letters To Buyers

[Date]

«AddressBlock»

«GreetingLine»

Thank you for your recent inquiry to my Web site. I hope that you have found the information in my Web site to be adequate to answer all your real estate questions pertaining to your property.

Please feel free to let me know any additional questions you may have about this listing, and I will be more than happy to provide the information to you.

[*Company Name*] has been helping families for many years in the [*Area Name*] area, and we take great pride in going the extra mile for all our real estate customers. We consider it an honor and a privilege to work with you on your real estate needs, and we look forward to helping you find your next home.

Again, thank you for your recent e-mail, and I look forward to hearing from you soon.

Yours truly,

[Agent Name]
[Agent Title]

Letters To Buyers

[Date]

«AddressBlock»

«GreetingLine»

I wanted to send you a quick thank you for the opportunity to show you properties today. It was a real pleasure and I enjoyed being able to meet you and your family. I do feel I have a better idea of the types of properties you are looking for, and I am setting up a search in our listing service that will notify you of any new listings with the criteria you have provided me. Once the system finds a listing that matches your criteria, it will send a copy of that listing for you to review. If it then becomes a property you have more interest in and would like to preview, please contact me at [*Phone*], and I will set up an appointment for us to look at the property.

Please understand that some listings sent to you through the Multiple Listing Search function will be listings with other agencies; however, you can still work through me in previewing or purchasing any of these properties.

Again, I appreciate the opportunity to show you properties today, and I feel certain we will be able to find the right home for you in the near future.

Yours truly,

[Agent Name]
[Agent Title]

Letters To Buyers

[Date]

«AddressBlock»

«GreetingLine»

Here are a few listings that I thought you might have an interest in looking at. It was a real pleasure meeting both of you today, and I appreciate the opportunity to assist you with your real estate needs. Please remember that I can show you any of the homes listed in this search, at no cost or fee to you.

I would also be happy to look at your home and give you my input and suggestions to help get your property sold. With interest rates at an all-time low, now is a perfect time to buy and sell real estate.

Again, thanks for calling my office, and let me know if you would like to look at any of the attached listings.

Yours truly,

[Agent Name]
[Agent Title]

Letters To Buyers

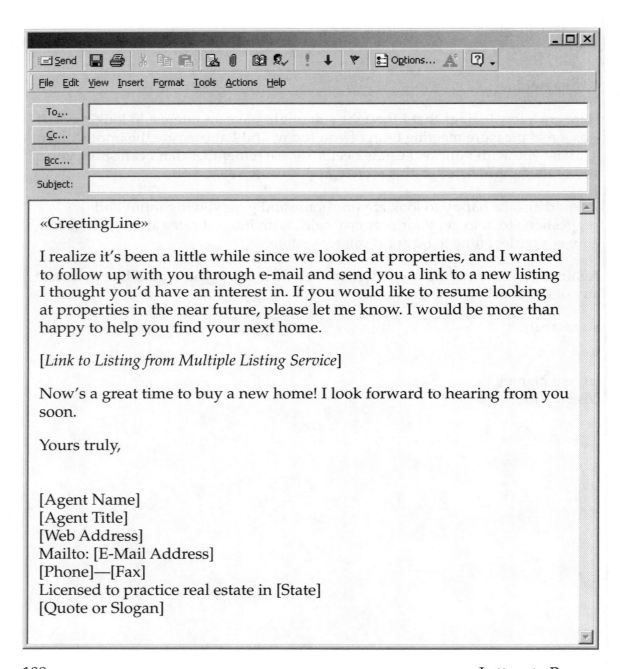

«GreetingLine»

I realize it's been a little while since we looked at properties, and I wanted to follow up with you through e-mail and send you a link to a new listing I thought you'd have an interest in. If you would like to resume looking at properties in the near future, please let me know. I would be more than happy to help you find your next home.

[*Link to Listing from Multiple Listing Service*]

Now's a great time to buy a new home! I look forward to hearing from you soon.

Yours truly,

[Agent Name]
[Agent Title]
[Web Address]
Mailto: [E-Mail Address]
[Phone]—[Fax]
Licensed to practice real estate in [State]
[Quote or Slogan]

Letters To Buyers

[Date]

«AddressBlock»

«GreetingLine»

I wanted to write a short note to you and explain my sorrow and disappointment for you that your recent loan transaction was denied. Please know that there are many factors that go into a loan approval in today's real estate economy and that some of the qualifications in approving buyers for home loans are out of the lender's hands. Don't take the denial on a personal level or let it discourage you from trying to buy a home in the near future. I believe that if you follow the suggestions from the lender on what needs to be done to become approved for a loan in the near future, you'll be able to do so.

I believe there's a better home for you and your family in the near future, and I hope that I can be a part of that real estate transaction.

In the meantime, if you have any questions about real estate, please keep me in mind. You know that I like to help you.

Yours truly,

[Agent Name]
[Agent Title]

Letters To Buyers

[Date]

«AddressBlock»

«GreetingLine»

I wanted to send a quick letter just to tell you that I know it can be discouraging when you're not approved for a home loan. Our office has witnessed many people like you who faced the same challenges, but diligently worked to make the improvements and suggestions from the lender to become qualified for home ownership status at a later time. I feel confident that you can make those necessary changes in a short period of time to reapply and become approved for a home loan.

I look forward to helping you in the future, and please call me any time you have questions.

Yours truly,

[Agent Name]
[Agent Title]

Letters To Buyers

[Date]

«AddressBlock»

«GreetingLine»

The attached [*Scan or Fax*] contains the executed documents on the property you are purchasing through me at [*Address*]. Congratulations, you now have an accepted contract on the property you want to purchase. You are now ready to move forward and finalize the necessary documents to close your loan. I'm sure [*Lender*] will be calling you with additional information and documents they will need for your home loan.

If there's anything I can do in the meantime to expedite this process, please do not hesitate to give me a call.

It's important that we remember [*Inspection Due Date*] as the date that all of our inspection reports must be turned over to the seller's agent regarding the property and any corrections or repairs that you request from the sellers. Please contact an inspection agency as soon as possible so that you can get this requirement fulfilled as soon as possible and before [*Inspection Due Date*].

I appreciate your business, and I look forward to a smooth and successful closing within the next month.

Yours truly,

[Agent Name]
[Agent Title]

Letters To Buyers

[Date]

«AddressBlock»

«GreetingLine»

It's been over a month since we closed on your real estate transaction, and I do hope that you are enjoying your new home. I wanted to write and ask you a quick favor that I would greatly appreciate. I am always looking for testimonial letters that I can include with presentations to use for buyers and sellers who are new to our area. A testimonial from you would be a big asset for my business. Any type of short note of recommendation would be greatly appreciated.

Thank you for your faith and support and for allowing me the opportunity to help you find your new home. It truly is satisfied clients like you and the referrals you send me that are the keys that help my business grow. A satisfied testimony from you would be a great addition to my presentation.

Again, thank you for your business and friendship. It's been a pleasure to serve you, and I look forward to working for you in the future. Enjoy your new home!

Yours truly,

[Agent Name]
[Agent Title]

Letters To Buyers

[Date]

«AddressBlock»

«GreetingLine»

I hope that you are enjoying your new home, and things are beginning to get back to normal. I wanted to write you a short note and tell you again how much I appreciate being able to work with you and finding your new home. I must admit that it was so much fun working with both of you on your transaction that in many ways it's a little sad that it's over with. However, I know that our paths will cross again and that our friendship will remain for many years to come.

As a self-employed real estate professional, one of the key ingredients for my success is from referrals from past clients, like you. It is so important for me to have others in the marketplace recommending my services as a real estate professional. If you know of people in the market wishing to buy or sell a home, please let them know about me, and see if I can have permission to contact them. It would be a great compliment and honor to handle your friend's real estate needs.

Again, thank you for allowing me the privilege of helping you with your real estate needs. I'm so glad that our paths have crossed and that I can now call you my friends. Please let me know if I can ever help or answer any real estate questions you may have.

Yours truly,

[Agent Name]
[Agent Title]

Letters To Buyers

[Date]

«AddressBlock»

«GreetingLine»

Thank you for your recent phone call about properties for sale in my area. I have enclosed some information about [*Name of Area*] as well as homes for sale in our marketplace matching the description that you provided me. You'll notice that some of the homes included in this group of listings are listed with other real estate agencies. However, I can still be your main point of contact for viewing any of these properties.

Remember that you can preview any of the properties online at [*Web Address*]. Our Web site has additional photos and virtual tours of many of our properties, along with other important information about each home for sale.

I look forward to meeting you and your family when you visit the area, and I hope the enclosed information is helpful. Again, thank you for allowing me to help you with your real estate needs during your potential move.

Yours truly,

[Agent Name]
[Agent Title]

Letters To Buyers

[Date]

«AddressBlock»

«GreetingLine»

I received your e-mail today about your need for information about [*Name of the Area*]. First, thank you for your inquiry to help you! I have included with this e-mail information about [*Name of the Area*] as well as homes for sale matching the description you provided me. You will notice that many of the homes listed for sale are with other real estate agents or agencies; however, I can still be your main point of contact for viewing any of these homes for sale.

Please let me know if there are any additional questions I can answer about our area that would be helpful in advance of your first visit. I have also included a few of my favorite Web links that provide a wealth of information about [*Name of the Area*].

I look forward to meeting you and your family should you make a visit to our area, and hope the enclosed information is helpful. Again, thank you for your e-mail, and I hope to hear from you soon.

Yours truly,

[Agent Name]
[Agent Title]

Letters To Buyers

[Date]

«AddressBlock»

«GreetingLine»

I do hope things are going well for you and your family, and I realize it's been a while since we have met. I wanted to let you know that the property I showed you at [*Address of Property*] has a new price. That's right, the sellers have reduced the price to [*New Price*]. If you still have an interest in this property, please let me know. I would be happy to show this home to you again if you would like to preview it for a second time. I have attached a Web link to the property for you to preview the information at your earliest convenience.

[*Address of Property*]

As always, thank you for providing me the opportunity to serve your real estate needs, and I hope to hear from you soon.

Yours truly,

[Agent Name]
[Agent Title]

Letters To Buyers

[Date]

«AddressBlock»

«GreetingLine»

I wanted to say thank you for taking time out of your busy schedule to visit my open house this past weekend at [*Address of Open House*]. I hope you enjoyed it and found that the additional information about the house was helpful for you. I have more photos and a virtual tour about this property online at my Web site [*Agent Web Address*]. I also have some excellent resources on my Web site for buyers and sellers that I believe you will find beneficial and helpful when you're ready to buy or sell your next home.

Again, thank you for visiting my open house, and please let me know if I can help you in any way with your real estate needs.

Yours truly,

[Agent Name]
[Agent Title]

Letters To Buyers

[Date]

«AddressBlock»

«GreetingLine»

I wanted to send you a quick note and tell you how much I appreciate the opportunity to serve as your buyer's representative on your next home purchase. As your buyer's agent, I promise and pledge to help you find a suitable home that fits your needs and is within your price range. One of my goals as your buyer's representative is to diligently work in finding a home that matches your description. My first step to achieve this goal is to set up a customized home search for you in our Multiple Listing Service. I have taken the information you have provided me and have created this customized search that will send you notification of new listings as they become available. Please know that I have widened and enlarged the search features so that you will get a better selection of properties to choose from. Please feel free to delete any listings that are of no interest to you; however, when you see a property that matches what you were looking for and is a home that you may want to preview in person, please let me know so that I can set up the necessary appointment.

It is also important for you to let me know or contact me as you find properties through the newspaper, as you drive around the area, visit open houses, etc. As your buyer's representative, it is important that you contact me first. I can then get the information for you and arrange for us to preview the home. If you do visit an open house, be sure to explain to the agent on duty that you are working with me and that I am representing you as a buyer's agent. Trust me, the representative on duty at the open house will appreciate knowing this in advance!

You've made the right decision in choosing me as your buyer's representative, and I appreciate and thank you for providing me this opportunity to serve your real estate needs. I feel certain we will find the right property you're looking for, and I promise to make the home buying transaction a pleasant experience.

Yours truly,

[Agent Name]
[Agent Title]

Letters To Buyers

[Date]

«AddressBlock»

«GreetingLine»

I know that it must be exciting for you to realize that we are so close to finalizing your documents on your new home. I also know that with all the excitement and last-minute details that we can sometimes overlook one of the most important parts of the transaction, "our final walk through." We will need to perform our final walk through before the closing at [*Time for Final Walk Through*]. I will have a checklist for you to use when we perform our final walk through.

Finally, our closing date is [*Date for Closing*], at [*Escrow Agency Location*], in [*City*] at [*Closing Time*].

As always, I appreciate your business, and please let me know if there is anything I can do between now and the closing.

Yours truly,

[Agent Name]
[Agent Title]

Letters To Buyers

[Date]

«AddressBlock»

«GreetingLine»

Now that our closing is final, I did want to write and apologize for the mix-up at the closing this week. Unfortunately, sometimes last-minute stuff can happen, and I apologize for all the craziness that took place. Most people would not have been so kind and understanding as you both were, and I appreciate the manner and professionalism with which you handled these problems.

As always, thank you for your business, and please let me know if I can help in the future.

Yours truly,

[Agent Name]
[Agent Title]

Letters To Buyers

[Date]

«AddressBlock»

«GreetingLine»

Yes, it's finally finished! To me it seems like yesterday that we started our home search for you. I am hopeful that you find your new home a delight and a treat to live in, and that your family will be able to make many wonderful memories there. It was such a pleasure to get to know both of you and I do feel as though I have made new friends during this process. Again, thank you!

I have enclosed a couple of business cards, and I would appreciate you passing on this information to anyone you know or hear about who may be interested in buying or selling real estate. As you know, my real estate business is dependent upon referrals from friends like you. Any help you can provide me in sending potential buyers or sellers my way is greatly appreciated.

Again, thank you for your business, and please know that I'm here long after the sale for any needs you might have or help you might need. Enjoy your new home!

Yours truly,

[Agent Name]
[Agent Title]

Letters To Buyers

[Date]

«AddressBlock»

«GreetingLine»

I am sorry things did not work out for the transaction on the home that you had hoped to purchase. Don't get discouraged, I believe there is a better home out there for you and your family.

Enclosed you will find an earnest money check for [*Amount of Check*], [*Check Number*] for the deposit you had placed on the property at [*Address*].

Thank you for allowing [*Name of Company*] the opportunity to serve your real estate needs. When you're ready to begin your home search again please know that I would love to assist and help you on your next transaction.

Yours truly,

[Agent Name]
[Agent Title]

Letters To Buyers

[Date]

«AddressBlock»

«GreetingLine»

As the old saying goes, "a day late and a dollar short," perhaps that best describes my situation on your recent transaction. However, I am glad you found a piece of property that fits your needs. I appreciated the opportunity you provided me to help you with your new home search, and I wish my efforts would have been more fruitful. Nevertheless, I am glad that you were able to find a property that matches your needs, and I want you to know I wish you the best of luck with your new home.

Please keep me in mind if I can ever help you with real estate needs in the future. Again, thank you, and I wish you the best of luck with your new home.

Yours truly,

[Agent Name]
[Agent Title]

Letters To Buyers

[Date]

«AddressBlock»

«GreetingLine»

Enclosed you will find a gift that I have included regarding your purchase on your home at [Address of Property]. This interactive CD-ROM/jump drive contains all of the important documents from your recent home purchase. I have taken the time to scan all of the documents from your recent transaction and made them available in this electronic format. Please keep this CD-ROM/jump drive in a safe place where it cannot be destroyed by fire or by other natural disasters. If for some reason you misplace the CD or cannot find it in the future, I will keep the files available for a short period of time and can provide you with a new copy. Please know that my copies of your transaction are stored securely on our company server database.

As always, thank you for providing me the opportunity to serve your real estate needs.

Yours truly,

[Agent Name]
[Agent Title]

Letters To Buyers

[Date]

«AddressBlock»

«GreetingLine»

Enclosed is the tax bill for the property you purchased through me last year. On the settlement statement at closing, the seller paid their portion of the taxes and you had a credit with taxes from January 1 through the day of closing. Therefore, you will be responsible for the taxes before (tax deadline date) to avoid any penalties. I know sometimes this seems a bit confusing, so please feel free to call me if you have any questions.

As always, thank you for providing me the opportunity to serve your real estate needs.

Yours truly,

[Agent Name]
[Agent Title]

Letters To Buyers

[Date]

«AddressBlock»

«GreetingLine»

I have listed below some important dates and obligations we have on the home you are purchasing at [*Address of Property*]. It is important that we meet all of the inspection dates to comply with the terms of the sales contract:

- All inspections completed   [Date]
- Financing approval   [Date]
- Other contingencies [List]   [Date]
- Closing   [Date]

Again, it is extremely important that we meet all of these dates on time so you will stay on track with your sales contract and our provided contingencies. If not, I will need to ask for an extension to your contract on the issues you feel you cannot comply with. Please note that it is better for us to try to fulfill the dates listed above before the time frame if possible. This will allow us plenty of time to respond to any problems that might arise.

As always, thank you for providing me the opportunity to serve your real estate needs. Please call me if you have any questions. I'll be in touch.

Yours truly,

[Agent Name]
[Agent Title]

Letters to Sellers

Keeping your clients abreast as to what is happening with their property for sale is one of the biggest responsibilities you have as a real estate professional. In my 32 years of experience as a real estate broker and sales associate, I have always tried to maintain regular contact with my clients and customers. Believe me, this continuous communication with my clients paid me big dividends as a real estate agent.

Real estate professionals work in a fast pace and hectic environment. This can play havoc on your good intentions of communicating with your clients regularly. I've tried to develop this chapter for you to have letters that you can use to communicate with your client/seller regardless of whether you have no activity, a lot of activity, or just need to do a quick follow-up to show you care about their needs. There are times some of the letters may require a little more work on your part to make them successful, such as adding the number of visits to a Web site, etc. However, I believe that if you follow a plan of action, implement the follow-up letters as well as phone calls and other personal visits, you will become a real estate hero in your seller's eyes even if their property does not sell.

Of course, your goal as a real estate professional is to sell each and every listing you have, but if you cannot sell your client's property, you still want them to appreciate and be satisfied with the service you provided while you had their listing contract.

Letters to Seller

Thank You Letter—#1

[Date]

«AddressBlock»

«GreetingLine»

Thank you for providing [*Company Name*] and me the opportunity to list your property on today's real estate market. I am honored that you have chosen my firm to help you sell your house. At this time we have taken the information you have provided us and entered the data into our Multiple Listing Service (MLS) where nearly [*Number of Agents in MLS*] local real estate agents have access when searching for properties for sale in [*Market Area*]. Besides marketing your property through our local MLS, your home will also be available on the World Wide Web through several top-rated home selling portals as well as our company Web site, [*Company Web Address*].

I have enclosed a property flyer for you to preview and to advise me of any additions or corrections that need to be made. At [*Company Name*], we pride ourselves on going above and beyond the call of duty for our clients and customers, and our main objectives and goals for you are as follows:

- *Outstanding customer service*
- *Help sell your real estate in the shortest time frame possible*
- *Help you achieve the maximum dollar amount for your real estate on today's market*

With over [*Years in Business*] years of experience and helping thousands of families with their real estate needs in [*Market Area*], you can rest assure that choosing [*Company Name*] for your real estate needs is the right decision!

Please feel free to call or e-mail for any questions you might have. My direct phone number is [*Agent Phone Number*], or you can reach me by e-mail at [*Agent E-Mail*].

As always, thank you for providing me the opportunity to serve your real estate needs.

Yours truly,

[Agent Name]
[Agent Title]

Thank You Letter—#2

[Date]

«AddressBlock»

«GreetingLine»

I would like to say thank you for allowing me to serve your real estate needs. I recognize the confidence and trust you have placed in my company and me, and I assure you that I will strive to give you the best service available in our area!

I have provided information to our local Multiple Listing Service® (MLS®) organization, which will give hundreds of other real estate agents in our area access to your property. This enables not only [*Agency Name*] to try to find a buyer, but also other companies as well. I do promise that I will do everything possible to qualify potential buyers before someone shows your property.

My goal is simple:

"To sell your home in the fastest time frame possible, with no problems, and to net you the most amount of money!"

If at any time you would like to visit with me concerning the marketing efforts of your property, please give me a call.

As always, thank you for providing me the opportunity to serve your real estate needs.

Yours truly,

[Agent Name]
[Agent Title]

Where Your Property Is Listed

[Date]

«AddressBlock»

«GreetingLine»

Again, I want to say thank you for your business and support in [*COMPANY NAME*] regarding your real estate needs. I wanted to share with you some of the marketing activities that are currently under way with your property I have listed. Currently, your property is being promoted on several online real estate classified Web sites throughout the World Wide Web. Your property is featured on web sites like REALTOR.com, Zillow.com, Truilia.com, Yahoo.com and many other web sites consumers visit to look for real estate for sale. Since the Internet is such a vast area to do business, you never know where our next buyer may come from.

(Note: Please feel free to add additional web sites you are currently using to promote your listings to in the body of this letter).

Customers and clients will sometimes ask about local print advertising and whether their property should be placed in the newspaper. Unfortunately, newspapers and magazines are not where buyers tend to come from today. According to the 2008 Profile of Home Buyers and Sellers by The National Association of REALTORS®, *87% of buyers begin their search online!* That number climbs to 94% of buyers between the ages of 24 and 34. Only a fraction of the respondents surveyed indicated that they use the newspaper to find homes for sale. I can also testify that I receive very few, if any, leads when print advertising is used.

Besides the sites noted above, I'm also busy promoting your property through video and PowerPoint on Web sites like YouTube, VodPod, Yahoo, and SlideShare. Please know I'm doing everything possible to find a buyer for your property, and I feel certain that I'll locate a buyer for your listing soon! If you ever have any ideas, suggestions, or comments, please feel free to call.

As always, thank you for providing me the opportunity to serve your real estate needs.

Yours truly,

[Agent Name]
[Agent Title]

Thank You—Expired Listing

[Date]

«AddressBlock»

«GreetingLine»

I wanted to take time out to write and thank you for the opportunity you provided me in listing your property over the last several months. I am saddened that I wasn't able to locate a buyer for you; however, I hope that you were pleased with my marketing efforts and realize that not every house sells every time. There are many variables and obstacles that can prohibit a home from selling. I still think you have a great property, a good product and I thought it was priced very attractively. Unfortunately I wasn't able to get the job done, and to that I say I'm sorry.

I wish you and your family the best of luck in the future. I hope that you can sell your property, and please always feel free to call me if you have any questions or need any help.

Yours truly,

[Agent Name]
[Agent Title]

Thank You—Expired Listing

[Date]

«AddressBlock»

«GreetingLine»

I wanted to write a short note and let you know how much I appreciated the opportunity you provided me in letting me try and sell your real estate. I'm sorry I was not able to find a buyer for your property. I still believe you have a wonderful home, and I only wish that I could have played a part in finding a buyer for it.

Let me know if I can help you in the future. Again, thanks for your business!

Yours truly,

[Agent Name]
[Agent Title]

Thank You— After a Completed Transaction

[Date]

«AddressBlock»

«GreetingLine»

I wanted to take time out of my day to write you a short letter and say thank you again for your faith and support you showed in [*COMPANY NAME*], and for providing me the opportunity to service your listing. I do hope that you were pleased with our marketing efforts and services during the course of our business relationship, and I hope that you will consider using our services again in the future. Satisfied clients like you and the referrals you send to me help grow my business.

If for any reason you have any real estate questions in the future [*Letter Name*], please do not hesitate to give me a call. Again, thank you for your business and friendship. It's been a pleasure to serve you.

Yours truly,

[Agent Name]
[Agent Title]

Seller Follow-Up Letters

Letter #1

[Date]

«AddressBlock»

«GreetingLine»

I realize that we have had your property listed for a little over one month now, and I wish I had better news to report. Unfortunately, some listings take longer to sell than other properties, and of course, the current economic conditions play a major role in how quickly properties will sell. Please know and understand that I am not discouraged in any way. I still have an optimistic outlook on the sale of your property and feel confident that we will find a buyer soon. In the meantime, please continue to make every effort at keeping your property in tip-top shape for a potential showing. You never know when we may have an interested prospect and keeping your property in the same marketable condition as the day I listed is very important.

As always, thank you for your business and your continued support for [*COMPANY NAME*]. Feel free to call me if you have any questions.

Yours truly,

[Agent Name]
[Agent Title]

Seller Follow-Up Letters

Letter #2

[Date]

«AddressBlock»

«GreetingLine»

Now that it has been 60 days since your property has been on the market, I believe it's time we consider the possibility of adjusting your price. Sometimes, a small price reduction can help jump-start activity and also lead to an accepted offer to purchase. If you would be interested in reducing the list price of your house, please call me and I'll prepare the necessary documentation to get the price changed in our Multiple Listing System and on our Web site.

As always, I thank you so much for your friendship and for your continued support for [*COMPANY NAME*].

Yours truly,

[Agent Name]
[Agent Title]

Seller Follow-Up Letters

Letter #3

[Date]

«AddressBlock»

«GreetingLine»

I "tweeted" about you today! Yes, you've heard the buzz and all the excitement around Twitter. I took the time today to tweet about your property, and what a great listing it is for potential buyers looking in the [*Area Name*] area.

Currently, I have [*Number of Twitter Followers*] people following me on Twitter who may know of someone interested in this type of property and/or who may re-tweet this information to their network of friends making our potential reach to consumers in the marketplace massive.

I realize many people in the social media may be way out in left-field; however, it is another marketing vehicle we can use to help expose your property to the most potential audience possible.

As always, thank you for your business. Feel free to call me if you have any questions. And, if you're on Twitter and we are not following each other already, I would love to get connected today.

Yours truly,

[Agent Name]
[Agent Title]

Seller Follow-Up Letters

Letter #4

[Date]

«AddressBlock»

«GreetingLine»

I wrote about you on my wall today! That's right. I posted a link and some pictures regarding your property on my Facebook wall today. Currently, I have approximately [*Number of Facebook Friends*] friends on my Facebook account who may read this post and preview the photos that I have placed on my wall. I wanted you to be aware that I am using a wide variety of marketing techniques (online and offline) to help expose your property to the widest audience possible. You never know where our buyer will come from.

If you have any questions, feel free to call me. If you are on Facebook and we're not friends, I would love to add you as a friend today. You can then go to my wall and see the post I made of your property.

As always, thank you for your business. I look forward to hearing from you soon.

Yours truly,

[Agent Name]
[Agent Title]

Seller Follow-Up Letters

Letter #5

[Date]

«AddressBlock»

«GreetingLine»

You made the list! That's right. Today, I posted your property on Craigslist! This is one of the fastest growing Internet online classified vehicles for selling stuff, including real estate. Many real estate professionals, including myself, are getting some good responses from Craigslist. There are many buyers who are out looking for properties on Craigslist, and now your property has been posted along with several exterior photos for potential consumers to preview. Keep in mind, any potential lead will have to go through me and be qualified financially prior to previewing your property.

In the meantime, if you have any questions, please feel free to contact me at [*Agent Phone Number*].

Again, it's just another way to hopefully find a potential buyer for your property.

Yours truly,

[Agent Name]
[Agent Title]

Seller Follow-Up Letters

Letter #6

[Date]

«AddressBlock»

«GreetingLine»

OPEN HOUSE—NOT MANY LOOKERS #1

Thank you for allowing me to hold your house open this past weekend. I'm sorry that we did not have a bigger turn out than we did. Open houses can sometimes be a little funny. It's either at one end of the spectrum or the other. Generally, you'll either have an excellent turn out with lots of buyers or very few folks attending.

Please don't get discouraged that our open house had such a small number. I still feel confident that we have a great product and that we have a potential buyer who will be looking at your property soon. In the meantime, let's remain optimistic and stay encouraged about selling your property. I'd love to try another open house in the near future. I'm sure we'll be in touch so let me know possible dates that will work for you.

As always, thank you for your business. I appreciate your friendship and support for [*COMPANY NAME*].

Yours truly,

[Agent Name]
[Agent Title]

Seller Follow-Up Letters

Open House—Not Many Lookers #2 Letter #7

[Date]

«AddressBlock»

«GreetingLine»

I'm sorry we didn't have better results with our open house this past weekend. I know that you went to a lot of trouble in getting everything ready for our big day. Don't be discouraged. Sometimes, open houses will not produce the kind of numbers that we would hope. I still feel confident that we have a great product and that we have a potential buyer who will be looking at your property soon. In the meantime, let's remain optimistic and stay encouraged about selling your property. I'd love to try another open house in the near future. I'm sure we'll be in touch so let me know possible dates that will work for you.

I appreciate your support, kindness, and patience. I look forward to a successful and quick closing soon.

Yours truly,

[Agent Name]
[Agent Title]

Seller Follow-Up Letters

Agent Open House Positive Response Letter #8

[Date]

«AddressBlock»

«GreetingLine»

Thank you for allowing me to hold an agent open house tour this past week. We had some excellent feedback from all of the agents who attended. Overall, the consensus of the agents was that we have a good product, and it seems to be priced competitively. Here are a few of the comments and suggestions that few of the agents made.

[*Insert Comments/Suggestions*].

I plan to call you in the next few days to discuss this report further and find out what you feel our next marketing strategy should be.

As always, thanks for your business and continued support for [*COMPANY NAME*].

Yours truly,

[Agent Name]
[Agent Title]

Seller Follow-Up Letters

Agent Open House—Need to Reduce Price

[Date]

«AddressBlock»

«GreetingLine»

Thank you for allowing me to conduct an agent open house tour. We had a lot of excellent feedback from the agents, and I appreciated their openness and honesty with regards to our marketing endeavors as well as the current list price. Unfortunately, many of the agents who toured your property believe that we might be asking a little too much in comparison to other properties that are currently for sale.

One reason I like to hold agent tours is to get their feedback, especially on price. Based on some of the comments, we probably should arrange a time that we can talk to discuss some possible solutions. Please let me know when a good time would be for me to come by and visit with you about this feedback.

As always, thank you for your business, and I look forward to hearing from you soon.

Yours truly,

[Agent Name]
[Agent Title]

E-mails to Seller
Offer to Purchase

«GreetingLine»

The attached [*Scan or Fax*] contains the offer to purchase we recently received on your property. Please take time to review the contract and sign and initial in the places indicated. As we discussed by telephone, I think this is an excellent offer on your property, and I support your decision in accepting the attached contract.

Again, if you have any questions regarding where to sign or initial, or about the sales contract in general, please do not hesitate to give me a call at [*Agent Phone Number*].

As always, it's a joy and a pleasure to serve your real estate needs. I'm excited about our new sales contract, and I look forward to a smooth closing

Yours truly,

[Agent Name]
[Agent Title]
[Web Address]
Mailto: [E-Mail Address]
[Phone]—[Fax]
Licensed to practice real estate in [State]
[Quote or Slogan]

E-mails to Seller
Offer to Purchase

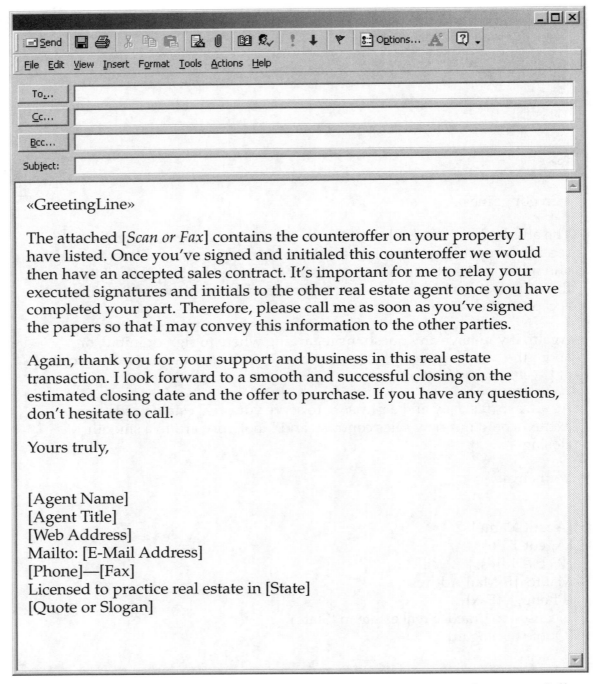

«GreetingLine»

The attached [*Scan or Fax*] contains the counteroffer on your property I have listed. Once you've signed and initialed this counteroffer we would then have an accepted sales contract. It's important for me to relay your executed signatures and initials to the other real estate agent once you have completed your part. Therefore, please call me as soon as you've signed the papers so that I may convey this information to the other parties.

Again, thank you for your support and business in this real estate transaction. I look forward to a smooth and successful closing on the estimated closing date and the offer to purchase. If you have any questions, don't hesitate to call.

Yours truly,

[Agent Name]
[Agent Title]
[Web Address]
Mailto: [E-Mail Address]
[Phone]—[Fax]
Licensed to practice real estate in [State]
[Quote or Slogan]

E-mails to Seller
Offer to Purchase

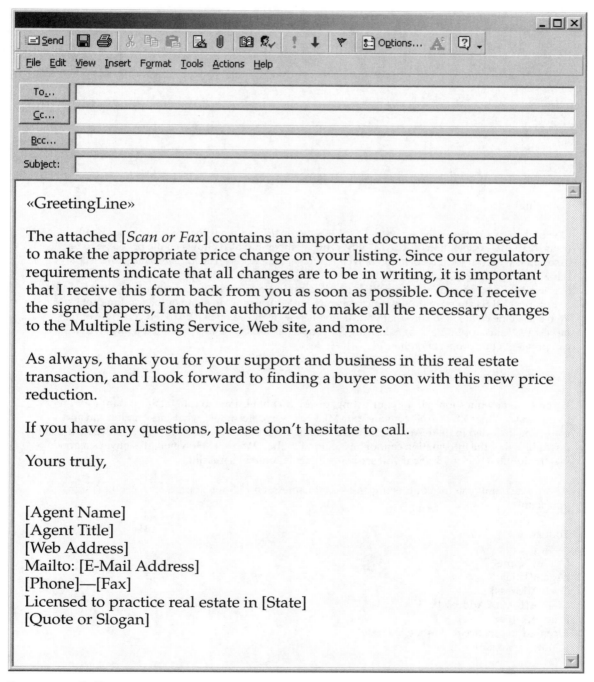

«GreetingLine»

The attached [*Scan or Fax*] contains an important document form needed to make the appropriate price change on your listing. Since our regulatory requirements indicate that all changes are to be in writing, it is important that I receive this form back from you as soon as possible. Once I receive the signed papers, I am then authorized to make all the necessary changes to the Multiple Listing Service, Web site, and more.

As always, thank you for your support and business in this real estate transaction, and I look forward to finding a buyer soon with this new price reduction.

If you have any questions, please don't hesitate to call.

Yours truly,

[Agent Name]
[Agent Title]
[Web Address]
Mailto: [E-Mail Address]
[Phone]—[Fax]
Licensed to practice real estate in [State]
[Quote or Slogan]

E-mails to Seller
Offer to Purchase

«GreetingLine»

One of the advantages of listing with [*COMPANY NAME*] and me is that we are proud members of the National Association of REALTORS®. This membership also allows us the privilege to be associated with our local association of REALTORS® [*Local Realtor® Association Name*], and as part of our association with [*Local Realtor® Association Name*] we can also belong to the local Multiple Listing Service (MLS) organization. Before this gets too complicated, just let me say that one of the benefits of our local MLS is to provide strategic placement of your listing on some of the top Internet listing Web sites. One of the Web sites that your listing is now featured on is REALTOR.com, one of the largest Web sites for home buyers looking for properties for sale. I have included a link so that you can preview your property online.

[*Web Address Link*]

If you have any questions about your listing, please do not hesitate to call. It's important for you to understand that REALTOR.com and our MLS have predetermined what information can and cannot be included in their Web site. If there is something not listed at REALTOR.com there's a good possibility that the information cannot be included in their Web site. However, it is always a good idea to double-check with me if you see some information that's missing.

As always, thank you for your listing and your business, and I hope to produce a "SOLD" sign for you soon!

Yours truly,

[Agent Name]
[Agent Title]
[Web Address]
Mailto: [E-Mail Address]
[Phone]—[Fax]
Licensed to practice real estate in [State]
[Quote or Slogan]

E-mails to Seller Number of Leads From Web Site

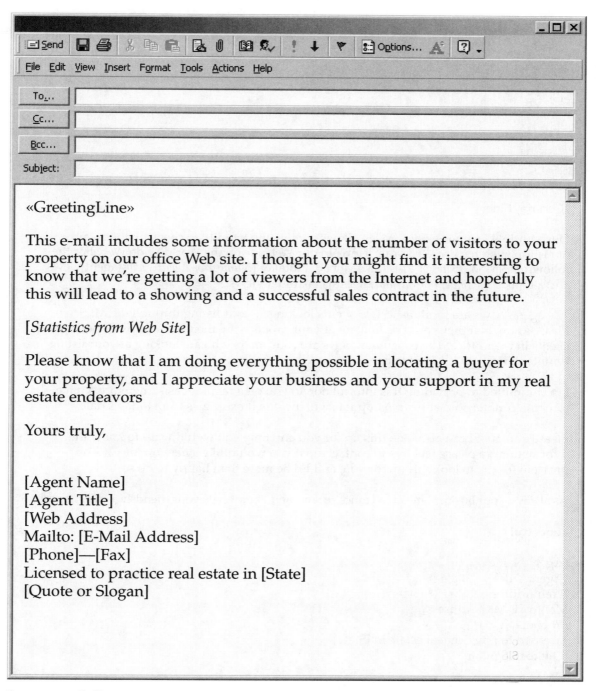

«GreetingLine»

This e-mail includes some information about the number of visitors to your property on our office Web site. I thought you might find it interesting to know that we're getting a lot of viewers from the Internet and hopefully this will lead to a showing and a successful sales contract in the future.

[*Statistics from Web Site*]

Please know that I am doing everything possible in locating a buyer for your property, and I appreciate your business and your support in my real estate endeavors

Yours truly,

[Agent Name]
[Agent Title]
[Web Address]
Mailto: [E-Mail Address]
[Phone]—[Fax]
Licensed to practice real estate in [State]
[Quote or Slogan]

E-mails to Seller Statistics from MLS

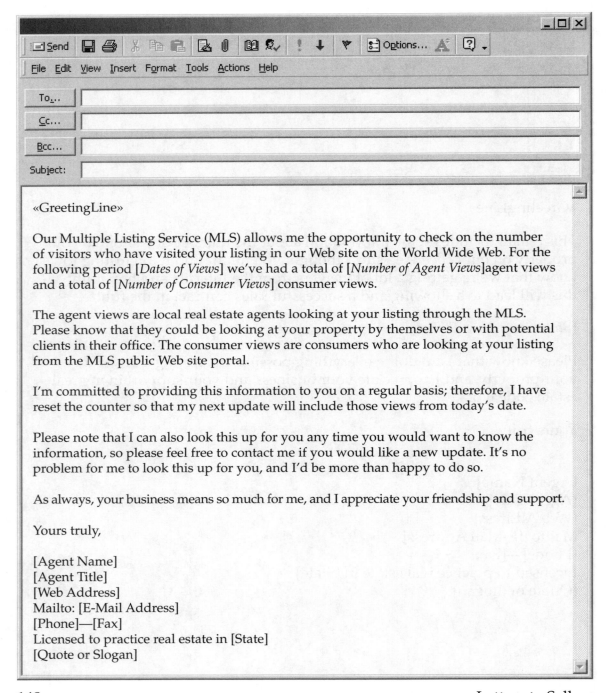

«GreetingLine»

Our Multiple Listing Service (MLS) allows me the opportunity to check on the number of visitors who have visited your listing in our Web site on the World Wide Web. For the following period [*Dates of Views*] we've had a total of [*Number of Agent Views*]agent views and a total of [*Number of Consumer Views*] consumer views.

The agent views are local real estate agents looking at your listing through the MLS. Please know that they could be looking at your property by themselves or with potential clients in their office. The consumer views are consumers who are looking at your listing from the MLS public Web site portal.

I'm committed to providing this information to you on a regular basis; therefore, I have reset the counter so that my next update will include those views from today's date.

Please note that I can also look this up for you any time you would want to know the information, so please feel free to contact me if you would like a new update. It's no problem for me to look this up for you, and I'd be more than happy to do so.

As always, your business means so much for me, and I appreciate your friendship and support.

Yours truly,

[Agent Name]
[Agent Title]
[Web Address]
Mailto: [E-Mail Address]
[Phone]—[Fax]
Licensed to practice real estate in [State]
[Quote or Slogan]

E-mails to Seller
Company Web Site Statistics

≡Send | **File** **Edit** **View** **Insert** **Format** **Tools** **Actions** **Help**

To...	
Cc...	
Bcc...	
Subject:	

«GreetingLine»

Here's a recent report I have attached from the Internet. This report provides you with the latest statistics of how many people are viewing your listing at [*Company Web Site*]. Of course, buyers can locate your property from many different areas on the World Wide Web and this is just one particular site with available statistics.

This report is just another way for me to stay in contact with you and let you know that I'm constantly monitoring the marketing efforts on your listing, and when I believe we should make some necessary changes I will always keep you abreast of those changes.

Again, thanks for your real estate business. Don't get discouraged, I feel confident we'll be locating a buyer soon.

Yours truly,

[Agent Name]
[Agent Title]
[Web Address]
Mailto: [E-Mail Address]
[Phone]—[Fax]
Licensed to practice real estate in [State]
[Quote or Slogan]

E-mails to Seller
Virtual Tour Link

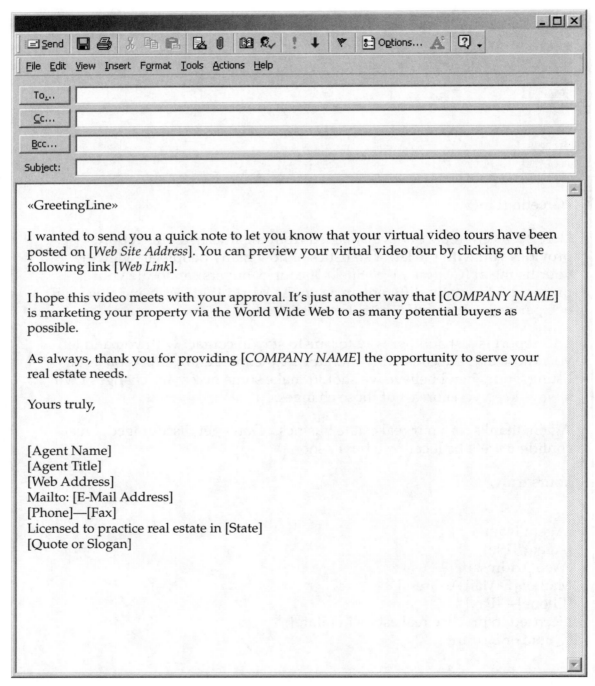

«GreetingLine»

I wanted to send you a quick note to let you know that your virtual video tours have been posted on [*Web Site Address*]. You can preview your virtual video tour by clicking on the following link [*Web Link*].

I hope this video meets with your approval. It's just another way that [*COMPANY NAME*] is marketing your property via the World Wide Web to as many potential buyers as possible.

As always, thank you for providing [*COMPANY NAME*] the opportunity to serve your real estate needs.

Yours truly,

[Agent Name]
[Agent Title]
[Web Address]
Mailto: [E-Mail Address]
[Phone]—[Fax]
Licensed to practice real estate in [State]
[Quote or Slogan]

E-mails to Seller Requesting Additional Documents

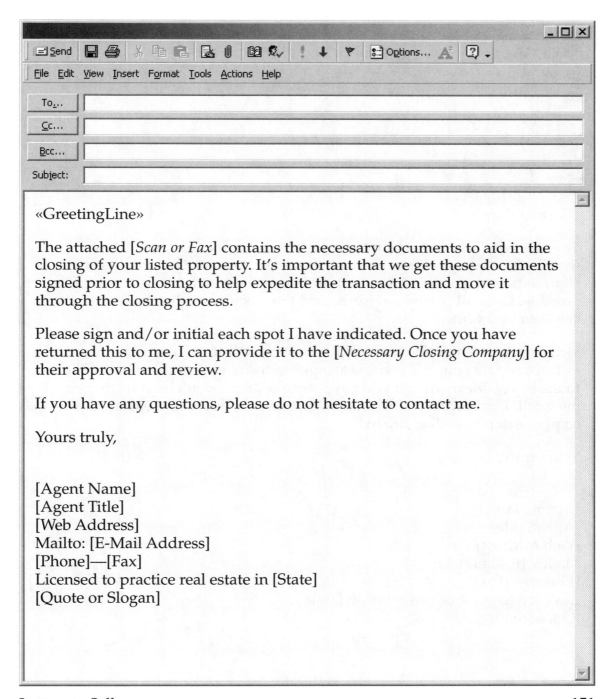

«GreetingLine»

The attached [*Scan or Fax*] contains the necessary documents to aid in the closing of your listed property. It's important that we get these documents signed prior to closing to help expedite the transaction and move it through the closing process.

Please sign and/or initial each spot I have indicated. Once you have returned this to me, I can provide it to the [*Necessary Closing Company*] for their approval and review.

If you have any questions, please do not hesitate to contact me.

Yours truly,

[Agent Name]
[Agent Title]
[Web Address]
Mailto: [E-Mail Address]
[Phone]—[Fax]
Licensed to practice real estate in [State]
[Quote or Slogan]

E-mails to Seller
Release of Earnest Money

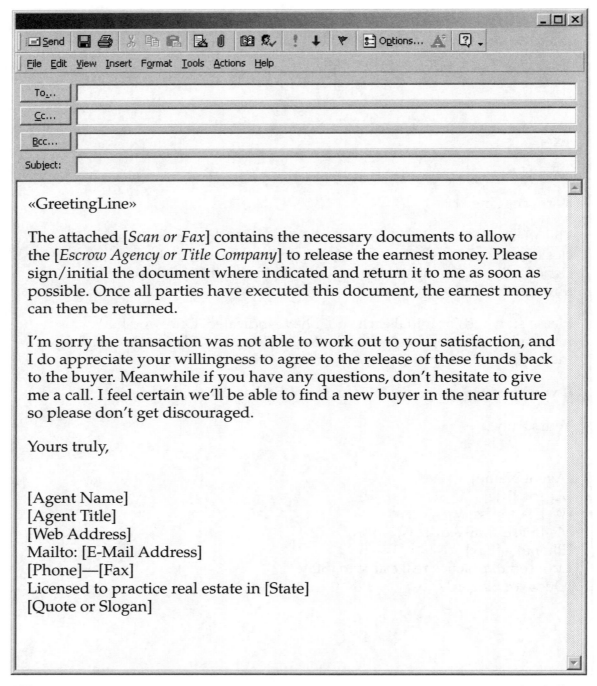

«GreetingLine»

The attached [*Scan or Fax*] contains the necessary documents to allow the [*Escrow Agency or Title Company*] to release the earnest money. Please sign/initial the document where indicated and return it to me as soon as possible. Once all parties have executed this document, the earnest money can then be returned.

I'm sorry the transaction was not able to work out to your satisfaction, and I do appreciate your willingness to agree to the release of these funds back to the buyer. Meanwhile if you have any questions, don't hesitate to give me a call. I feel certain we'll be able to find a new buyer in the near future so please don't get discouraged.

Yours truly,

[Agent Name]
[Agent Title]
[Web Address]
Mailto: [E-Mail Address]
[Phone]—[Fax]
Licensed to practice real estate in [State]
[Quote or Slogan]

E-mails to Seller
Contract Didn't Go Through

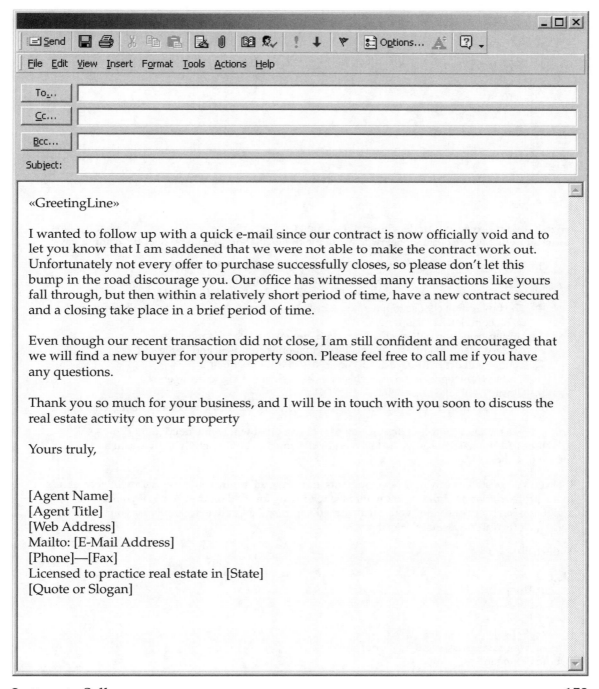

«GreetingLine»

I wanted to follow up with a quick e-mail since our contract is now officially void and to let you know that I am saddened that we were not able to make the contract work out. Unfortunately not every offer to purchase successfully closes, so please don't let this bump in the road discourage you. Our office has witnessed many transactions like yours fall through, but then within a relatively short period of time, have a new contract secured and a closing take place in a brief period of time.

Even though our recent transaction did not close, I am still confident and encouraged that we will find a new buyer for your property soon. Please feel free to call me if you have any questions.

Thank you so much for your business, and I will be in touch with you soon to discuss the real estate activity on your property

Yours truly,

[Agent Name]
[Agent Title]
[Web Address]
Mailto: [E-Mail Address]
[Phone]—[Fax]
Licensed to practice real estate in [State]
[Quote or Slogan]

E-mails to Seller
Property is Now Under
Contract

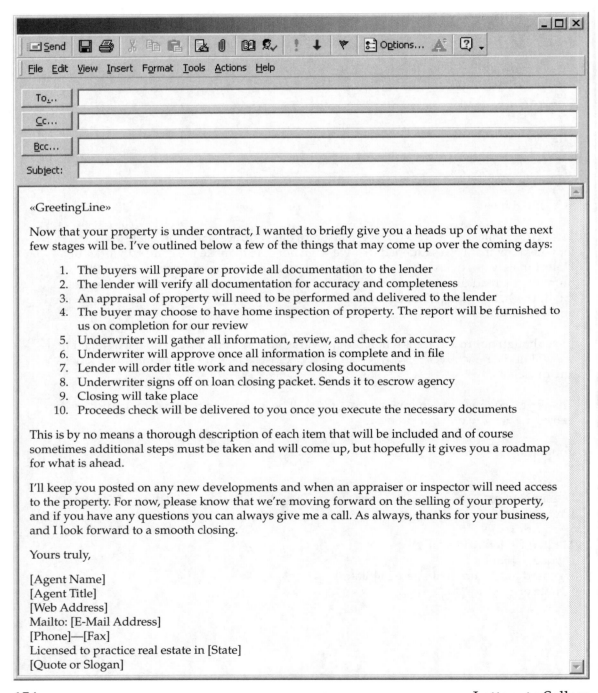

«GreetingLine»

Now that your property is under contract, I wanted to briefly give you a heads up of what the next few stages will be. I've outlined below a few of the things that may come up over the coming days:

1. The buyers will prepare or provide all documentation to the lender
2. The lender will verify all documentation for accuracy and completeness
3. An appraisal of property will need to be performed and delivered to the lender
4. The buyer may choose to have home inspection of property. The report will be furnished to us on completion for our review
5. Underwriter will gather all information, review, and check for accuracy
6. Underwriter will approve once all information is complete and in file
7. Lender will order title work and necessary closing documents
8. Underwriter signs off on loan closing packet. Sends it to escrow agency
9. Closing will take place
10. Proceeds check will be delivered to you once you execute the necessary documents

This is by no means a thorough description of each item that will be included and of course sometimes additional steps must be taken and will come up, but hopefully it gives you a roadmap for what is ahead.

I'll keep you posted on any new developments and when an appraiser or inspector will need access to the property. For now, please know that we're moving forward on the selling of your property, and if you have any questions you can always give me a call. As always, thanks for your business, and I look forward to a smooth closing.

Yours truly,

[Agent Name]
[Agent Title]
[Web Address]
Mailto: [E-Mail Address]
[Phone]—[Fax]
Licensed to practice real estate in [State]
[Quote or Slogan]

Letter after the closing—
Fast Sale

[Date]

«AddressBlock»

«GreetingLine»

We did it, it closed! Wow, I wish all my properties could sell so quickly, but unfortunately that's not the case. It is exciting that we were able to find a buyer so fast for your property, and I hope that you too were pleased with this quick turnaround.

I also wanted to say thank you again for your faith and support you showed in [*COMPANY NAME*] and for providing me the opportunity to service your listing. It is satisfied clients like you and the referrals you send to me that help my business grow.

If for any reason you have any real estate questions in the future [*Letter Name*], please do not hesitate to give me a call. Again, thank you for your business and friendship. It's been a pleasure to serve you.

Yours truly,

[Agent Name]
[Agent Title]

Letter after the Closing—
Took a While for Sale

[Date]

«AddressBlock»

«GreetingLine»

I wish I could have sent you this letter several months ago, but unfortunately sometimes certain real estate listings take a while to sell. The good news is we finally got it done! Words cannot express my sincere appreciation for you remaining loyal and believing in my marketing efforts to find a buyer for your property. Thank you!

The faith and support you showed in [COMPANY NAME] and the opportunity you provided me to service your listing is something I will always treasure. Satisfied clients like you and the referrals you send to me are the key ingredients that help my business grow. Any referrals you send my way in the future will be greatly appreciated.

If for any reason you have any real estate questions [Letter Name], please do not hesitate to give me a call. Again, thank you for your business and friendship. It's been a pleasure to serve you!

Yours truly,

[Agent Name]
[Agent Title]

Letter after the Closing— Asking for testimony

[Date]

«AddressBlock»

«GreetingLine»

I hope you're enjoying your new home! I wanted to write you a quick note to ask a favor of you. As you know, referrals from past clients and customers play a large part in the success of my business. Many times my new prospects would like to know a little bit more about me, and/or hear from other satisfied clients and customers. I was hoping you would be kind enough to write a short letter of recommendation for me that I could include with my presentations. This information would be priceless for me to include when I am visiting with customers who do not know me. Just a short note promoting me as your real estate agent would be helpful.

I would also like to remind you to remember me if you know of someone in the market wishing to buy or sell real estate.

Again, thanks for letting me serve your real estate needs. It was a real joy and a pleasure to work with you.

Yours truly,

[Agent Name]
[Agent Title]

Letter after the Closing— Asking for testimony

[Date]

«AddressBlock»

«GreetingLine»

Can you believe it's been three months since I sold your house? Wow, time goes by quickly. I hope you have settled into your new home and all is well for you! I do appreciate your business, and I hope we can work together on another real estate transaction in the future.

Much of my business is from referrals from past clients like you as well as friends and family members. Referrals are a major contributor to the success of my business. However, there are times when I work with out-of-town clients or people who just don't know me. For those instances, it is helpful for me to have testimonial letters to show these prospects how others have viewed my services. I thought of you, [*Letter Name*], and wondered if you would send me a brief testimonial letter that I could use in my marketing material. If this is something you could do for me, I would appreciate it. If you prefer not to, I understand.

Again, thank you for providing me the opportunity to help you with your real estate needs.

Yours truly,

[Agent Name]
[Agent Title]

Letter after the Closing— General Follow up

[Date]

«AddressBlock»

«GreetingLine»

I realize your house has been for sale for a while. I'm also sure you have legitimate concerns about why it hasn't sold. Unfortunately, several factors can contribute to this situation. Normally, the most important issue is price, and adjusting the price will always help. Another issue that plays a major role is the type of marketing features associated with the property. In other words, can we offer something of "value" to the prospective buyers so that they will choose our house over one offered by the competition? One idea is to offer a home warranty program to the new buyers. This is an excellent feature that covers many problems that can occur after the closing. This warranty gives the buyers peace of mind that if something does break down or go wrong, they may have insurance to cover it. I have enclosed information about home warranties for you. Please review this and decide if this is a marketing benefit you might want to offer. Keep in mind that there is no obligation to do this, it's just a suggestion to help with marketing your real estate.

I do appreciate the opportunity to serve your real estate needs, and don't hesitate to call me if you have any more questions about this home warranty program.

Yours truly,

[Agent Name]
[Agent Title]

Letter after the Closing— Thank you for extending listing

[Date]

«AddressBlock»

«GreetingLine»

Just a note to say thank you for extending your listing with me. I appreciate your continued faith and support in me and in [*Agency Name*]. Please know that I am using every avenue possible to secure a buyer for you, and I feel certain that a SOLD sign will be here soon. I realize how much a sale means to you.

Again, thanks for letting me serve your real estate needs.

Yours truly,

[Agent Name]
[Agent Title]

Letter after the Closing— Thank you for extending listing

[Date]

«AddressBlock»

«GreetingLine»

Just a note to say thank you for extending your listing with me. Wow, your continued faith and support in me and in [*Agency Name*] is appreciated. Thank you!

I want you to know that I am using every effort possible to find a buyer for your property. I realize how much a sale means to you.

Please call me if you have any questions, and again, thanks for letting me serve your real estate needs.

Yours truly,

[Agent Name]
[Agent Title]

Letter after the Closing— Seller listed with another firm

[Date]

«AddressBlock»

«GreetingLine»

Although I know that you have chosen another company to list your home for sale, I wish you the best of luck. Please keep me in mind if I can help in the future.

Again, thank you for giving me the opportunity to visit with you on your real estate needs.

Yours truly,

[Agent Name]
[Agent Title]

Letter after the Closing— General Follow up

[Date]

«AddressBlock»

«GreetingLine»

It's now been over 100 days since you first listed your real estate with me. As I have mentioned before, I know that as time goes by it can become discouraging to wonder why your property has not sold. Again, there are many answers to this question, and, unfortunately, trying to pinpoint the problem is not always easily done.

Please know that I am doing everything possible to expedite a sale for you, and always feel free to share any ideas or suggestions you might have for marketing your property.

As always, thank you for providing me the opportunity to serve your real estate needs.

Yours truly,

[Agent Name]
[Agent Title]

Letter after the Closing— Thank You for Adjusting Price

[Date]

«AddressBlock»

«GreetingLine»

I wanted to say thank you for agreeing to adjust your price on the property I have listed. I believe this price drop will have a positive impact on my marketing efforts. I'll keep you posted on the feedback I receive from agents and potential clients about our new price.

As always, thank you for providing me the opportunity to serve your real estate needs, and please don't hesitate to call me if you have any questions.

Yours truly,

[Agent Name]
[Agent Title]

Letter after the Closing— General Follow up

[Date]

«AddressBlock»

«GreetingLine»

Enclosed you will find some small business cards with your property photo and a brief description about your real estate for sale. As with any marketing plan, the key to a successful sale is to create as much interest as possible. This marketing idea is one good way to carry out that goal. Many of my clients like to have these cards to give out to friends and coworkers. It's a great way to help spread the word about your house, and it might even lead to a potential buyer. Let me know if you need a few more cards, and I will be glad to print out another sheet for you.

As always, thank you for providing me the opportunity to serve your real estate needs, and if we both think positive I know a SOLD sign will be here soon!

Yours truly,

[Agent Name]
[Agent Title]

Letter after the Closing— Returning Documents

[Date]

«AddressBlock»

«GreetingLine»

Enclosed you will find the documents you provided me for your listing at [*Address of Property*]. I appreciate your letting me borrow these documents during the listing period. They were very helpful to our office staff and me.

As always, thank you for providing me the opportunity to serve your real estate needs. Please let me know if I can help you in the future.

Yours truly,

[Agent Name]
[Agent Title]

Letter after the Closing— Agreement to End Listing

[Date]

«AddressBlock»

«GreetingLine»

This letter will serve as our agreement to end your listing contract with [*Agency Name*]. I am sorry that you wish to withdraw your listing with our company now. My goal is to sell every listing I have, but unfortunately this does not always happen. I appreciate your business, and I hope you will consider [*Agency Name*] in the future should the need arise.

Good luck, and again, thank you for allowing [*Agency Name*] to serve you during the time we had your listing.

Yours truly,

[Agent Name]
[Agent Title]

E-Mails and Letters to Other Agents

I t is important to communicate with our friends and colleagues as much as it is with clients and customers. Having a good rapport and good relationships with those we work with can make our jobs much easier in the long term.

The art of sending a short thank you card, note, or e-mail has almost gone by the wayside for many sales associates. I believe it is important for you to take the time and correspond with your real estate friends and associates, especially when they have sold one of your properties, shown one of your homes, or simply provided you with an act of kindness.

Taking the time to acknowledge others will set you apart from the typical real estate associate. In this chapter I have tried to provide a wide variety of short messages that can be used with e-mail or blank note cards to send to other agents in your marketplace. Although these pieces of correspondence have been specifically designed for use with e-mail or note cards they can still be applicable and used in a normal letter format.

It feels good to have someone say *thank you*, and this chapter will help you do just that for your friends and colleagues.

I can live for two months on a good compliment.
—Mark Twain

E-mail Messages to Other Agents

Price Reduction—#1

File Edit View Insert Format Tools Actions Help

To...

Cc...

Bcc...

Subject:

«GreetingLine»

I wanted to inform you that my listing at [*Property Address*] has recently had a price reduction from [*Old Price*] to [*New Price*]. This is an excellent listing with many quality features, and I believe that this new price is a great buy on today's market. If you have anyone who may be interested in looking at this listing, please be sure to keep this in mind.

Again, thanks for your time, and I always appreciate any support you can provide in showing my listings.

[*Link to Listing*]

Yours truly,

[Agent Name]
[Agent Title]
[Web Address]
Mailto: [E-Mail Address]
[Phone]—[Fax]
Licensed to practice real estate in [State]
[Quote or Slogan]

E-mail Messages to Other Agents

Price Reduction—#2

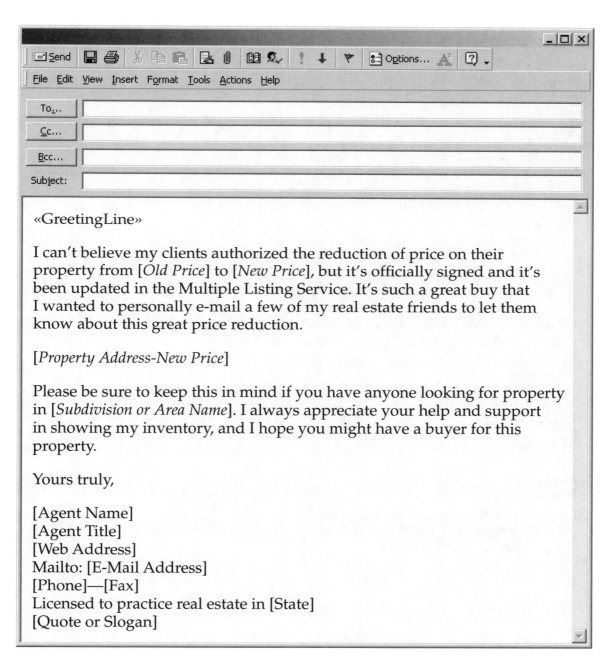

«GreetingLine»

I can't believe my clients authorized the reduction of price on their property from [*Old Price*] to [*New Price*], but it's officially signed and it's been updated in the Multiple Listing Service. It's such a great buy that I wanted to personally e-mail a few of my real estate friends to let them know about this great price reduction.

[*Property Address-New Price*]

Please be sure to keep this in mind if you have anyone looking for property in [*Subdivision or Area Name*]. I always appreciate your help and support in showing my inventory, and I hope you might have a buyer for this property.

Yours truly,

[Agent Name]
[Agent Title]
[Web Address]
Mailto: [E-Mail Address]
[Phone]—[Fax]
Licensed to practice real estate in [State]
[Quote or Slogan]

E-mail Messages to Other Agents

Took New Listing at Lower Price

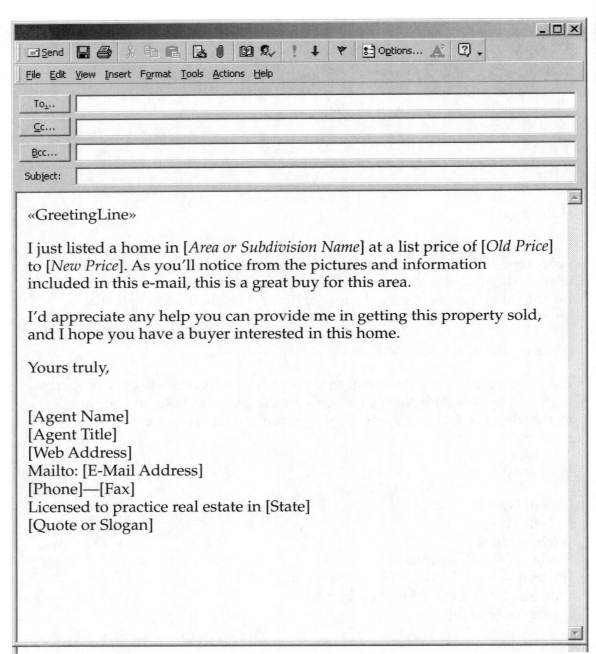

«GreetingLine»

I just listed a home in [*Area or Subdivision Name*] at a list price of [*Old Price*] to [*New Price*]. As you'll notice from the pictures and information included in this e-mail, this is a great buy for this area.

I'd appreciate any help you can provide me in getting this property sold, and I hope you have a buyer interested in this home.

Yours truly,

[Agent Name]
[Agent Title]
[Web Address]
Mailto: [E-Mail Address]
[Phone]—[Fax]
Licensed to practice real estate in [State]
[Quote or Slogan]

E-mail Messages to Other Agents

Agent Open House—#1

File Edit View Insert Format Tools Actions Help

To...

Cc...

Bcc...

Subject:

«GreetingLine»

I wanted to let you know that I'm having an agent open house this [*Date*] from [*Time*] to [*Time*]. I'll be serving food and having some great prizes that you can win by attending my agent open house.

[*Property Address*] [*Time and Date*] [*Door Prizes*]

This is a very nice home, and I'd like for you to take a few minutes out of your busy schedule to come by and take a look. I believe at this price we can sell this listing to someone very quickly.

I hope to see you at the open house, and I thank you in advance for your support and your business friendship.

Yours truly,

[Agent Name]
[Agent Title]
[Web Address]
Mailto: [E-Mail Address]
[Phone]—[Fax]
Licensed to practice real estate in [State]
[Quote or Slogan]

E-mail Messages to Other Agents

Agent Open House—#2

«GreetingLine»

Can I buy you lunch this [*Date of Agent Open House*] between [*Time of Agent Open House*]. Yes, I'm holding an agent open house at [*Address*]. I'll be serving a delicious meal and will be giving away some great door prizes.

I do hope you can attend this agent open house, because this property is priced below market value (in my opinion) and should sell fast.

I appreciate your time and thank you in advance for stopping by my agent open house. I look forward to seeing you [*Date and Time*] at [*Location*]

Yours truly,

[Agent Name]
[Agent Title]
[Web Address]
Mailto: [E-Mail Address]
[Phone]—[Fax]
Licensed to practice real estate in [State]
[Quote or Slogan]

E-mail Messages to Other Agents

Met Agent at Convention

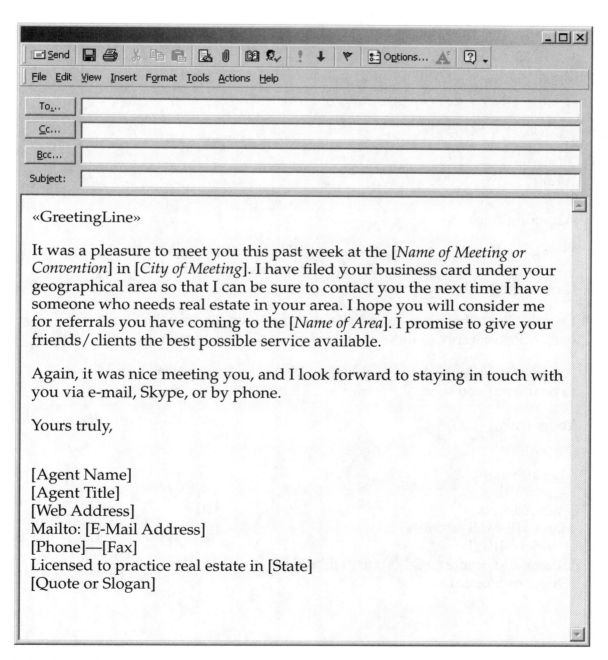

«GreetingLine»

It was a pleasure to meet you this past week at the [*Name of Meeting or Convention*] in [*City of Meeting*]. I have filed your business card under your geographical area so that I can be sure to contact you the next time I have someone who needs real estate in your area. I hope you will consider me for referrals you have coming to the [*Name of Area*]. I promise to give your friends/clients the best possible service available.

Again, it was nice meeting you, and I look forward to staying in touch with you via e-mail, Skype, or by phone.

Yours truly,

[Agent Name]
[Agent Title]
[Web Address]
Mailto: [E-Mail Address]
[Phone]—[Fax]
Licensed to practice real estate in [State]
[Quote or Slogan]

E-mail Messages to Other Agents

Thanks for Showing Listing

«GreetingLine»

Thank you for showing my listing at [*Address of Property*] this week. I hope your showing went well, and if there is any extra information I can provide for you, please let me know.

I would like to hear any comments you and your clients have about this listing. Please reply to this e-mail at your earliest convenience.

Again, thanks for showing my listing, [*Showing Agent's Name*], and I hope to hear from you soon.

Yours truly,

[Agent Name]
[Agent Title]
[Web Address]
Mailto: [E-Mail Address]
[Phone]—[Fax]
Licensed to practice real estate in [State]
[Quote or Slogan]

E-mail Messages to Other Agents

Wrote Offer But Did Not Work Out

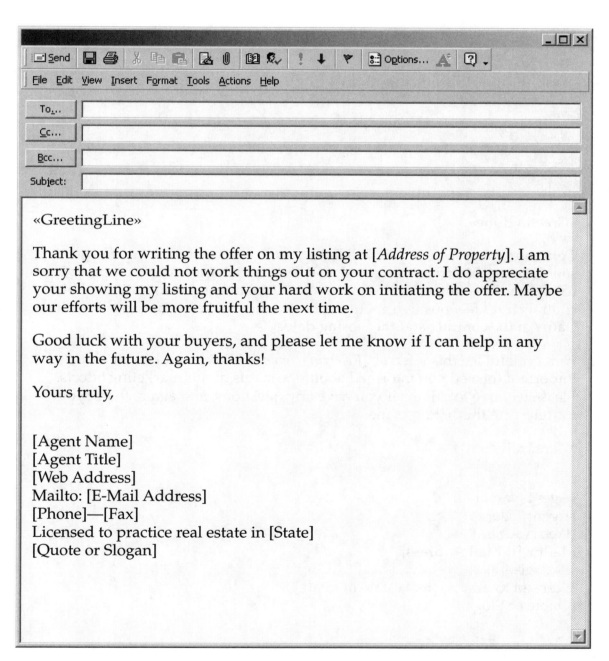

«GreetingLine»

Thank you for writing the offer on my listing at [*Address of Property*]. I am sorry that we could not work things out on your contract. I do appreciate your showing my listing and your hard work on initiating the offer. Maybe our efforts will be more fruitful the next time.

Good luck with your buyers, and please let me know if I can help in any way in the future. Again, thanks!

Yours truly,

[Agent Name]
[Agent Title]
[Web Address]
Mailto: [E-Mail Address]
[Phone]—[Fax]
Licensed to practice real estate in [State]
[Quote or Slogan]

E-mail Messages to Other Agents

Informing Referring Agent of Seller's Future Closing

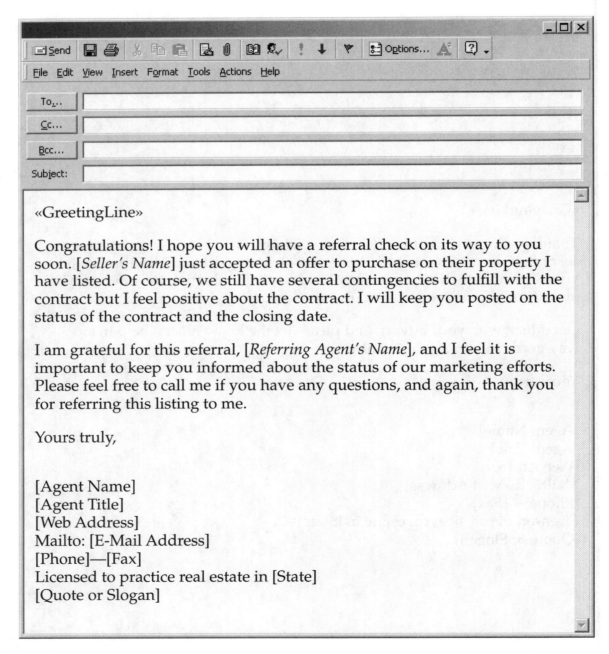

«GreetingLine»

Congratulations! I hope you will have a referral check on its way to you soon. [*Seller's Name*] just accepted an offer to purchase on their property I have listed. Of course, we still have several contingencies to fulfill with the contract but I feel positive about the contract. I will keep you posted on the status of the contract and the closing date.

I am grateful for this referral, [*Referring Agent's Name*], and I feel it is important to keep you informed about the status of our marketing efforts. Please feel free to call me if you have any questions, and again, thank you for referring this listing to me.

Yours truly,

[Agent Name]
[Agent Title]
[Web Address]
Mailto: [E-Mail Address]
[Phone]—[Fax]
Licensed to practice real estate in [State]
[Quote or Slogan]

E-mail Messages to Other Agents

Informing Referring Agent of Status with Buyer

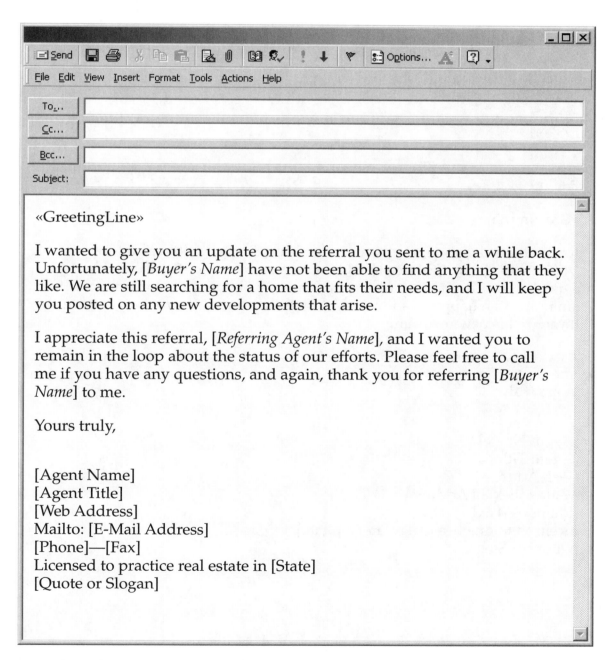

«GreetingLine»

I wanted to give you an update on the referral you sent to me a while back. Unfortunately, [*Buyer's Name*] have not been able to find anything that they like. We are still searching for a home that fits their needs, and I will keep you posted on any new developments that arise.

I appreciate this referral, [*Referring Agent's Name*], and I wanted you to remain in the loop about the status of our efforts. Please feel free to call me if you have any questions, and again, thank you for referring [*Buyer's Name*] to me.

Yours truly,

[Agent Name]
[Agent Title]
[Web Address]
Mailto: [E-Mail Address]
[Phone]—[Fax]
Licensed to practice real estate in [State]
[Quote or Slogan]

E-mail Messages to Other Agents

Skype Address

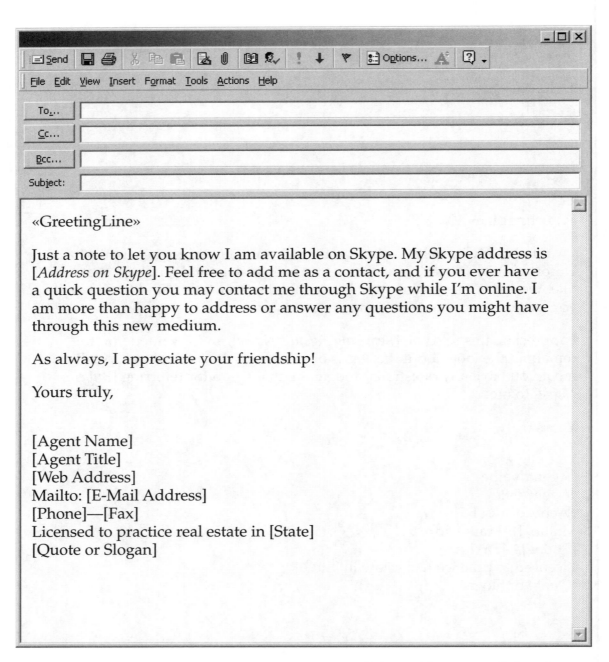

«GreetingLine»

Just a note to let you know I am available on Skype. My Skype address is [*Address on Skype*]. Feel free to add me as a contact, and if you ever have a quick question you may contact me through Skype while I'm online. I am more than happy to address or answer any questions you might have through this new medium.

As always, I appreciate your friendship!

Yours truly,

[Agent Name]
[Agent Title]
[Web Address]
Mailto: [E-Mail Address]
[Phone]—[Fax]
Licensed to practice real estate in [State]
[Quote or Slogan]

E-mail Messages to Other Agents

Join My Social Network

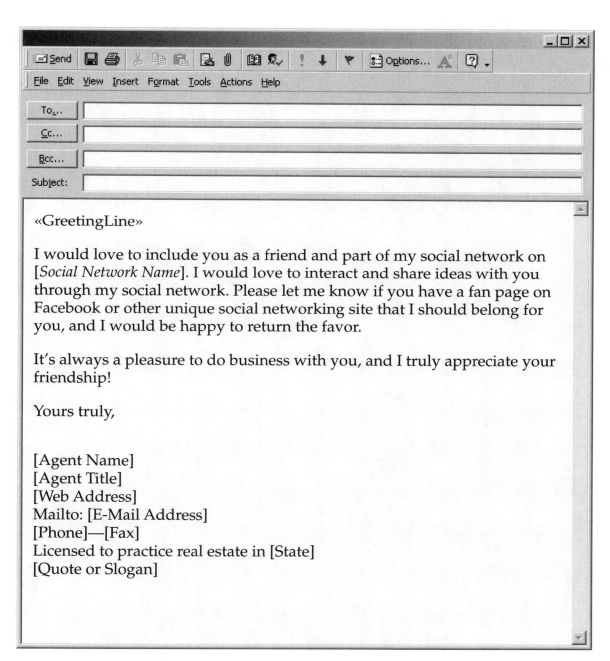

«GreetingLine»

I would love to include you as a friend and part of my social network on [*Social Network Name*]. I would love to interact and share ideas with you through my social network. Please let me know if you have a fan page on Facebook or other unique social networking site that I should belong for you, and I would be happy to return the favor.

It's always a pleasure to do business with you, and I truly appreciate your friendship!

Yours truly,

[Agent Name]
[Agent Title]
[Web Address]
Mailto: [E-Mail Address]
[Phone]—[Fax]
Licensed to practice real estate in [State]
[Quote or Slogan]

Letters to Vendors

In this section, Letters to Vendors, you will find several documents that can be used for corresponding and communicating with those people you come in contact with regularly. The letters you will find in this section can be used as stand-alone letters with your company or personal stationery; however, you might consider using them as handwritten forms with a blank, card stock thank you piece. People love handwritten notes, and it's never a bad idea to take the extra time and write out notes and letters to compliment someone you know. You can also use some of the templates in this section as e-mail messages.

Letters or E-Mails to vendors

Quick Closing by Lender/ Loan Officer

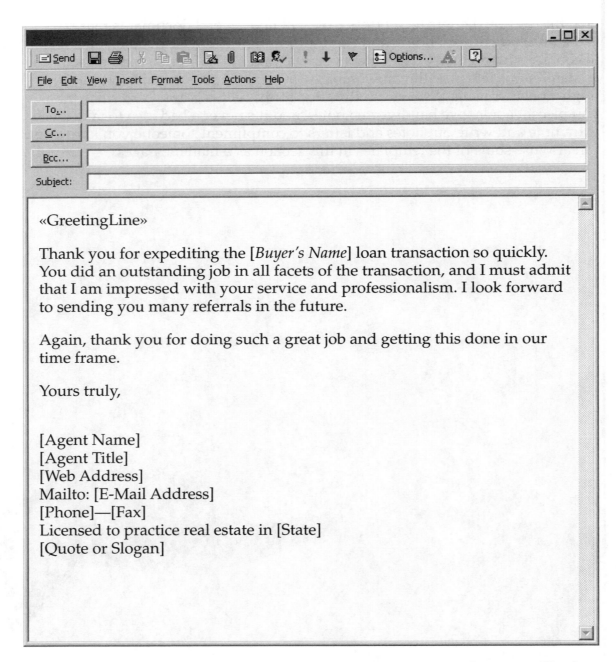

«GreetingLine»

Thank you for expediting the [*Buyer's Name*] loan transaction so quickly. You did an outstanding job in all facets of the transaction, and I must admit that I am impressed with your service and professionalism. I look forward to sending you many referrals in the future.

Again, thank you for doing such a great job and getting this done in our time frame.

Yours truly,

[Agent Name]
[Agent Title]
[Web Address]
Mailto: [E-Mail Address]
[Phone]—[Fax]
Licensed to practice real estate in [State]
[Quote or Slogan]

Letters or E-Mails to vendors

Loan That Took a Little Longer than Usual

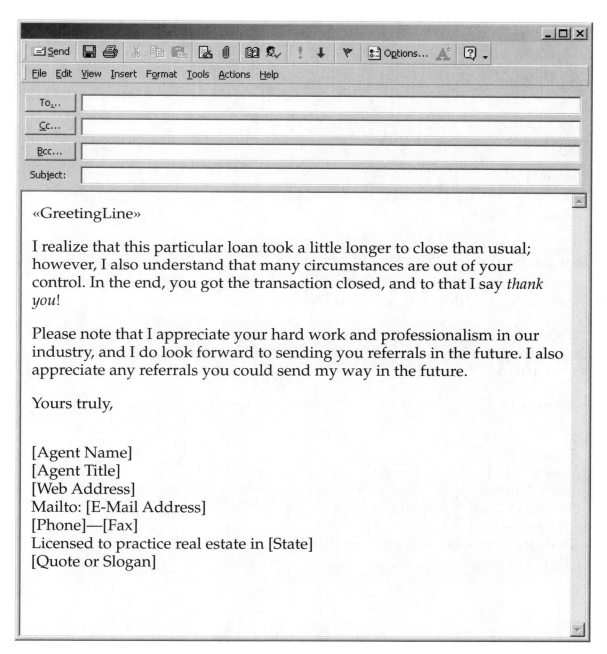

«GreetingLine»

I realize that this particular loan took a little longer to close than usual; however, I also understand that many circumstances are out of your control. In the end, you got the transaction closed, and to that I say *thank you*!

Please note that I appreciate your hard work and professionalism in our industry, and I do look forward to sending you referrals in the future. I also appreciate any referrals you could send my way in the future.

Yours truly,

[Agent Name]
[Agent Title]
[Web Address]
Mailto: [E-Mail Address]
[Phone]—[Fax]
Licensed to practice real estate in [State]
[Quote or Slogan]

Letters or E-Mails to vendors

To a Closing Agent

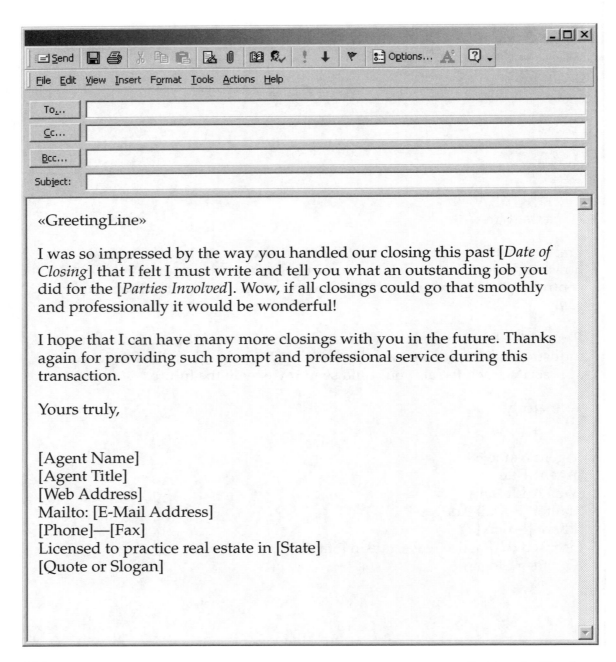

«GreetingLine»

I was so impressed by the way you handled our closing this past [*Date of Closing*] that I felt I must write and tell you what an outstanding job you did for the [*Parties Involved*]. Wow, if all closings could go that smoothly and professionally it would be wonderful!

I hope that I can have many more closings with you in the future. Thanks again for providing such prompt and professional service during this transaction.

Yours truly,

[Agent Name]
[Agent Title]
[Web Address]
Mailto: [E-Mail Address]
[Phone]—[Fax]
Licensed to practice real estate in [State]
[Quote or Slogan]

Letters or E-Mails to vendors

To Vendor Who Provided Service

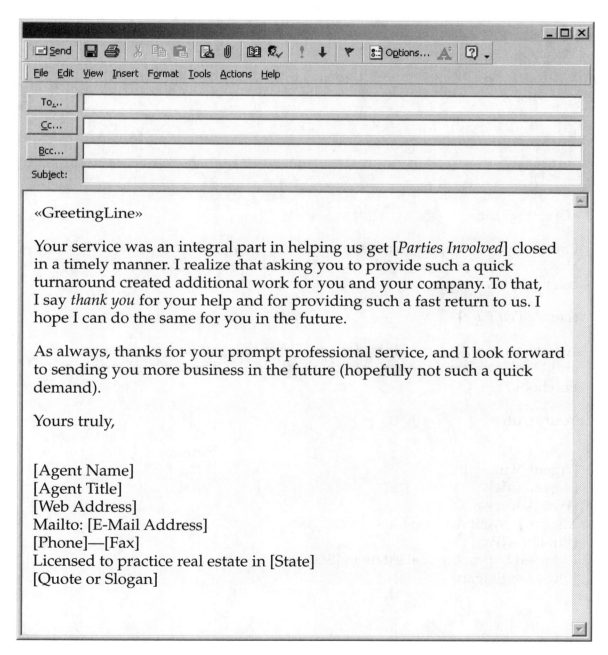

«GreetingLine»

Your service was an integral part in helping us get [*Parties Involved*] closed in a timely manner. I realize that asking you to provide such a quick turnaround created additional work for you and your company. To that, I say *thank you* for your help and for providing such a fast return to us. I hope I can do the same for you in the future.

As always, thanks for your prompt professional service, and I look forward to sending you more business in the future (hopefully not such a quick demand).

Yours truly,

[Agent Name]
[Agent Title]
[Web Address]
Mailto: [E-Mail Address]
[Phone]—[Fax]
Licensed to practice real estate in [State]
[Quote or Slogan]

Letters or E-Mails to vendors

Facebook Exchange

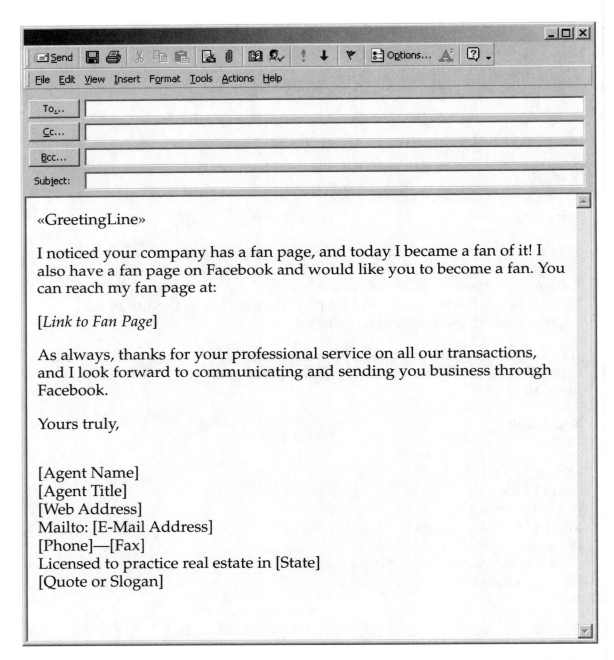

«GreetingLine»

I noticed your company has a fan page, and today I became a fan of it! I also have a fan page on Facebook and would like you to become a fan. You can reach my fan page at:

[*Link to Fan Page*]

As always, thanks for your professional service on all our transactions, and I look forward to communicating and sending you business through Facebook.

Yours truly,

[Agent Name]
[Agent Title]
[Web Address]
Mailto: [E-Mail Address]
[Phone]—[Fax]
Licensed to practice real estate in [State]
[Quote or Slogan]

Letter—Thank You for Speaking at Meeting

[Date]

«AddressBlock»

«GreetingLine»

It was a joy to have you speak at our [*Name of Organization*] meeting today. I appreciated your talk and learned a lot about [*Speech Topic*] that I did not know.

I realize your time is valuable. Again, thank you for contributing your time and knowledge in making our meeting such a success. I hope that we can have you back again in the near future.

Yours truly,

[Agent Name]
[Agent Title]

Follow-Up Letters

First Year Anniversary Letter

[Date]

«AddressBlock»

«GreetingLine»

Happy Anniversary!

Can you believe it's been one full year since the purchase of your home? Wow, time does go by quickly. I hope that your home has been a joy to you and your family this past year and that it is still the ideal place for you to enjoy and grow into for many years to come.

My business depends on referrals from friends like you. I have enclosed several business cards for you to hand out should you know of someone interested in buying or selling real estate.

I am now offering a FREE service to past customers and clients on what the estimated value is of the property they have purchased from me. This report is my way of helping you track your home's investment and saying *thanks* for your business. During this meeting I would also be happy to suggest any improvements that would assist in improving the value of your property.

Again, *Happy Anniversary* on the purchase of your home, and please know that I am here long after the sale for any needs you might have.

Yours truly,

[Agent Name]
[Agent Title]

Second Year Anniversary Letter

[Date]

«AddressBlock»

«GreetingLine»

Happy Anniversary!

Yes, it's now two years since you bought your home. I'm sure your home is fulfilling your family's needs, and is a place you can call home. The real joy and satisfaction I receive with my career is helping families like yours find a home they can enjoy for many years.

Are you receiving my e-mail newsletter? If your e-mail address has changed or if you are not receiving my monthly e-mail newsletter, please let me know and I can add you to the list.

Again, *Happy Anniversary* on the purchase of your home, and please know that I am here long after the sale for any needs you might have.

Yours truly,

[Agent Name]
[Agent Title]

Third Year Anniversary Letter

[Date]

«AddressBlock»

«GreetingLine»

Happy Anniversary!

Yes, it's been three years since you purchased your home from me. I hope your home is fulfilling your family's needs and is a place you all can call home. If you need more room or have a desire to relocate in the near future, please let me know. I would love to help you on your next real estate transaction. Now is a great time to buy and sell. Call me for information on today's real estate market.

Don't forget to notify me of your e-mail address. I would love to include you in my monthly newsletter list; the newsletter is full of information about what homes are selling for in the area, tips on saving money, and much more. You can notify me of your e-mail address (or change) at [*Agent E-Mail*].

Again, *Happy Anniversary* on the purchase of your home, and please know that I am here long after the sale for any needs you might have.

Yours truly,

[Agent Name]
[Agent Title]

Fourth Year Anniversary Letter

[Date]

«AddressBlock»

«GreetingLine»

Happy Fourth Anniversary!

No, I could not forget your anniversary! Can you believe it's been four full years since the purchase of your home? Wow, time does go by quickly. I hope that your home has been a joy to you and your family this past year and that it is still the ideal place for you and your family.

Again, *Happy Anniversary* on the purchase of your home, and please know that I am here long after the sale for any needs you might have.

Yours truly,

[Agent Name]
[Agent Title]

Fifth Year Anniversary Letter

[Date]

«AddressBlock»

«GreetingLine»

Happy Anniversary!

There are two parts of my business that are rewarding to me. The first is a satisfied client who uses my services or recommends me to friends for their real estate needs. The second gratifying aspect of my business is when past clients purchase a home they enjoy and stay there for a long time. Congratulations! This is the fifth anniversary of your home buy. I know I have said this in previous letters but time does go by quickly! I appreciated the opportunity to work with you on your home buy five years ago, and I hope all is going well with you.

Again, *Happy Anniversary* on the purchase of your home, and let me know if I can help in the future. Thanks!

Yours truly,

[Agent Name]
[Agent Title]

Sixth Year Anniversary Letter

[Date]

«AddressBlock»

«GreetingLine»

Happy Anniversary!

It's time for my annual congratulations letter, and this is year number six! I know I mention this every year, but time does go by quickly! It seems like yesterday that we closed on your home purchase. I am so glad you are still enjoying your home. If you would like to have an updated price evaluation on the equity in your home based on the current market conditions, I would be glad to do that for you. There's no charge, and it does not take long to complete. I appreciated the opportunity to work with you six years ago on your home buy, and I hope all is going well with you.

Again, *Happy Anniversary* on the purchase of your home, and let me know if I can help in the future. Thanks!

Yours truly,

[Agent Name]
[Agent Title]

Seventh Year Anniversary Letter

[Date]

«AddressBlock»

«GreetingLine»

Happy Anniversary!

Seven is a good number, and did you know it has been seven years since you purchased your home from me? Wow, to me it seems like yesterday that we closed on your home purchase. I am thrilled that you are still in your home, and I hope that it is still as warm and happy today as the first day you moved in. However, if you might be thinking about making a move and would like to have an updated price evaluation on the equity in your home based on the current market conditions, I would be glad to do that for you. There's no charge, and it does not take long to complete. I appreciated the opportunity to work with you seven years ago on your home buy, and I hope all is going well with you.

Again, *Happy Anniversary* on the purchase of your home, and let me know if I can help in the future. Thanks!

Yours truly,

[Agent Name]
[Agent Title]

Tax Form Letter

[Date]

«AddressBlock»

«GreetingLine»

I hope your holidays were joyous, and the New Year is off to a great start. I know that you will be preparing your tax returns during the next few months, so I have enclosed a copy of your settlement statement from this past year. Don't forget that there are many good tax-deductible items on this statement that you may be able to use this year when preparing your return. Please be sure to consult your tax advisor for more information about which closing costs are permissible for consideration on your taxes.

As always, I appreciate your business, and please feel free to call me any time with your real estate questions.

Yours truly,

[Agent Name]
[Agent Title]

PR Letters

Letter from Broker Announcing New Licensee

[Date]

«AddressBlock»

«GreetingLine»

[*Agency Name*] is pleased to announce the affiliation of [*Agent's Name*] to our company. [*Agent's Name*] has just completed an extensive training course to complete and pass the state licensing exam. [*Agency Name*] has also provided a detailed training program for [*Agent's Name*], and [*he/she*] is now ready to serve you with your real estate needs.

[*Agency Name*] has been helping families with their real estate needs since [*Year Agency Opened*]. You can visit our Web site at [*Web Address*] and find out more information about [*Agency Name*].

I hope you will consider [*Agent's Name*] for all your real estate needs. Also, encourage any friends, family members, or coworkers to consider [*Agent's Name*] for their real estate needs too.

Thank you for your time, and I hope [*Agent's Name*] will hear from you soon.

Yours truly,

[Agent Name]
[Agent Title]

Letter from Broker Announcing New Licensee

[Date]

«AddressBlock»

«GreetingLine»

[Agency Name] is proud to announce the affiliation of [Agent's Name] to our staff. [Agent's Name] has just completed all of the necessary requirements by [State] to receive [his/her] license, and we are excited to have [him/her] be a part of our team.

I hope you will consider using [Agent's Name] for any future real estate needs and allow [him/her] the opportunity to show you [Agency Name]'s aggressive marketing plan.

For a complete listing of homes for sale and other information about [Agency Name], visit our Web site at [Web Address].

Thank you for your time, and I hope [Agent's Name] will hear from you soon.

Yours truly,

[Agent Name]
[Agent Title]

Letter Announcing New Career

[Date]

«AddressBlock»

«GreetingLine»

I wanted to write you a brief note and tell you some exciting news about my career change. I am now working as a real estate professional for [*Agency Name*]. After completing my coursework, passing the appropriate exams, and completing my company sales training, I am now ready to help with your real estate needs.

Please feel free to contact me with any of your real estate requests. Also, please keep me in mind if you know of someone who is interested in buying or selling real estate. One of my biggest needs is referrals of customers from friends like you.

Finally, I have a Web site address you can visit at [*Web Address—Company or Personal*]. This Web site offers the opportunity for your property to be marketed 24 hours a day, 7 days a week! According to the *2008 National Association of REALTORS® Profile of Home Buyers and Sellers*, 87% of consumers used the Internet as a source to find homes to buy. At [*Agency Name*], we can offer you this type of service, and much more!

I appreciate your friendship, and I hope to help you or your friends with your real estate needs soon.

Yours truly,

[Agent Name]
[Agent Title]

Agent Completed Class

[Date]

«AddressBlock»

«GreetingLine»

Recently I completed [*Name of Class*]. This class dealt primarily with [*Type of Class*] issues in our real estate industry. I have a commitment to maintain an involvement with my real estate profession and to further my knowledge in this business that I enjoy so much. Most of all, I want you to know that I take educational classes for clients like you, so that when a need arises, you know you can count on me to be ready and prepared to help.

I appreciate your friendship. If you know of someone in the market to buy or sell a home, please give them my business card. Don't forget, you can visit my Web site at [*Web Address*] to view homes for sale in our area and find good real estate information.

My business is dependent on referrals and support from people like you, [*Letter Name*]. Thanks!

Yours truly,

[Agent Name]
[Agent Title]

Agent Completed Course/ Designation

[Date]

«AddressBlock»

«GreetingLine»

I wanted to write you a short note and tell you about a new real estate designation I just completed, [*Name of Course*]. I continue to take real estate educational courses as often as possible so I can stay ahead of the many changes in my industry. More importantly, I know that when it comes time to help friends like you with your real estate needs, I can give you the professional service you deserve.

I hope everything is going well for you, and please let me know if I can help with any real estate needs in the future.

By the way, my Web site address is [*Web Address*]. The site offers good information for buying and selling real estate as well as the capability to search listings currently for sale. Thanks for your time!

Yours truly,

[Agent Name]
[Agent Title]

Congratulations on Job Promotion

[Date]

«AddressBlock»

«GreetingLine»

Congratulations on your recent job promotion! I know you will be excellent in this new position, and your company picked the right person. This is a great honor, and I know you are excited and proud of the new challenge.

Good luck with your new role, and again, congratulations!

Yours truly,

[Agent Name]
[Agent Title]

Affiliated With New Real Estate Company

[Date]

«AddressBlock»

«GreetingLine»

I have some exciting news that I wanted to share with you about my real estate career. I am now associated with [*Company Name*]. I believe this move provides many new opportunities for me and my customers and clients, and I am very excited about the future.

I've enclosed my new business card for your future reference. Please call me for any real estate needs you have, and remember my Web address and e-mail address have not changed. Feel free to visit my Web site whenever you need to search for local homes listed for sale and to get other timely real estate information.

I appreciate your friendship, [*Letter Name*], and I hope you will continue to support me at [*Real Estate Company Name*]. Thank you!

Yours truly,

[Agent Name]
[Agent Title]

Affiliated with New Real Estate Company

[Date]

«AddressBlock»

«GreetingLine»

I wanted to write a short note and let you know that I am now affiliated with [*Company Name*]. After a lot of soul-searching and research I knew that it was best for me to pursue a new real estate agency to further my real estate career. [*Company Name*] provides a wide variety of tools and resources that will not only benefit me but also my clients and customers like you. I hope that I can count on you for future real estate business with my new affiliation at [*Company Name*].

It is good friends like you and the referrals you send me that helped my real estate career get better and better each year. Thank you so much for remembering me and mentioning my name whenever you hear of someone who needs to buy or sell real estate. Your referrals are always appreciated!

I have included several of my new business cards for you for future reference.

Again, thank you for your friendship and your business, and please let me know if I can help you with any real estate needs.

Yours truly,

[Agent Name]
[Agent Title]

Referral Letters/E-Mails

Thanks for Referral— Another Agent

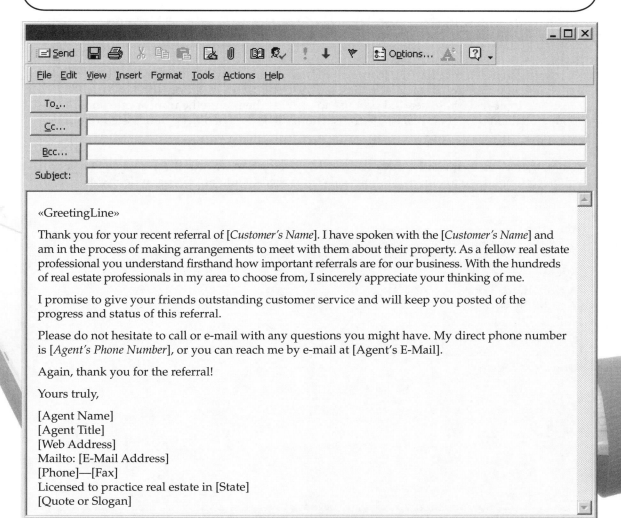

«GreetingLine»

Thank you for your recent referral of [*Customer's Name*]. I have spoken with the [*Customer's Name*] and am in the process of making arrangements to meet with them about their property. As a fellow real estate professional you understand firsthand how important referrals are for our business. With the hundreds of real estate professionals in my area to choose from, I sincerely appreciate your thinking of me.

I promise to give your friends outstanding customer service and will keep you posted of the progress and status of this referral.

Please do not hesitate to call or e-mail with any questions you might have. My direct phone number is [*Agent's Phone Number*], or you can reach me by e-mail at [Agent's E-Mail].

Again, thank you for the referral!

Yours truly,

[Agent Name]
[Agent Title]
[Web Address]
Mailto: [E-Mail Address]
[Phone]—[Fax]
Licensed to practice real estate in [State]
[Quote or Slogan]

Referral From Another Customer/Client #1

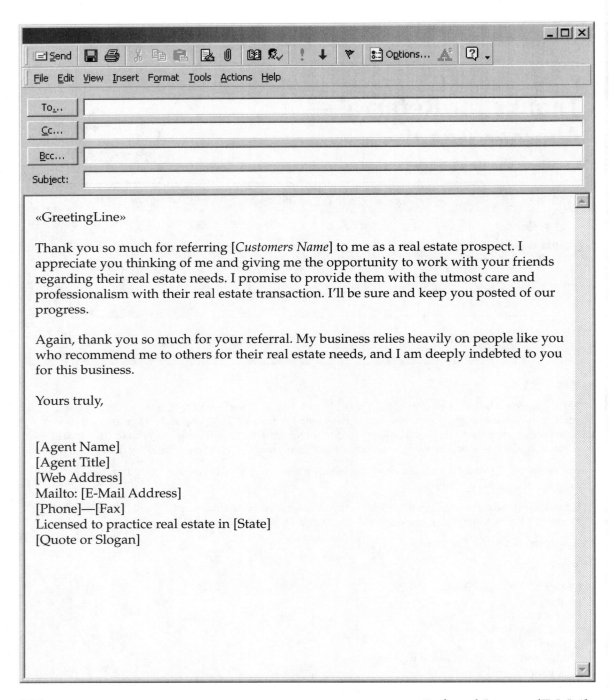

«GreetingLine»

Thank you so much for referring [*Customers Name*] to me as a real estate prospect. I appreciate you thinking of me and giving me the opportunity to work with your friends regarding their real estate needs. I promise to provide them with the utmost care and professionalism with their real estate transaction. I'll be sure and keep you posted of our progress.

Again, thank you so much for your referral. My business relies heavily on people like you who recommend me to others for their real estate needs, and I am deeply indebted to you for this business.

Yours truly,

[Agent Name]
[Agent Title]
[Web Address]
Mailto: [E-Mail Address]
[Phone]—[Fax]
Licensed to practice real estate in [State]
[Quote or Slogan]

Referral From Another Customer/Client #2

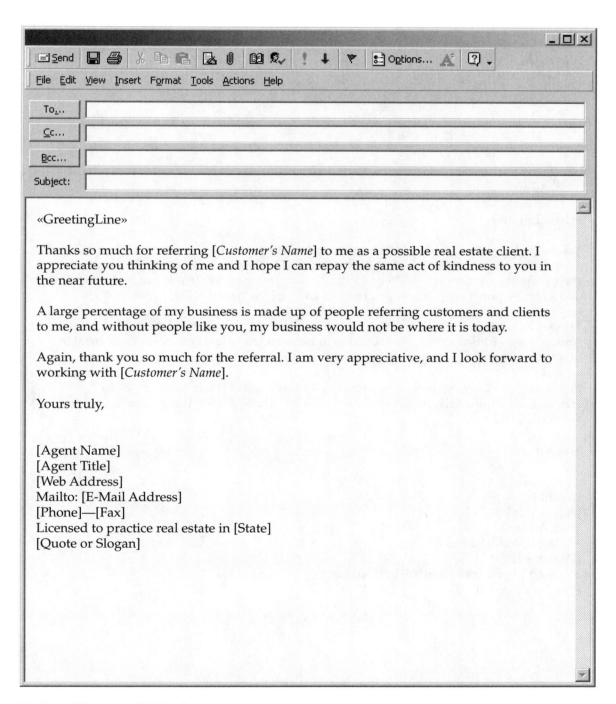

«GreetingLine»

Thanks so much for referring [*Customer's Name*] to me as a possible real estate client. I appreciate you thinking of me and I hope I can repay the same act of kindness to you in the near future.

A large percentage of my business is made up of people referring customers and clients to me, and without people like you, my business would not be where it is today.

Again, thank you so much for the referral. I am very appreciative, and I look forward to working with [*Customer's Name*].

Yours truly,

[Agent Name]
[Agent Title]
[Web Address]
Mailto: [E-Mail Address]
[Phone]—[Fax]
Licensed to practice real estate in [State]
[Quote or Slogan]

Thank You after Closing

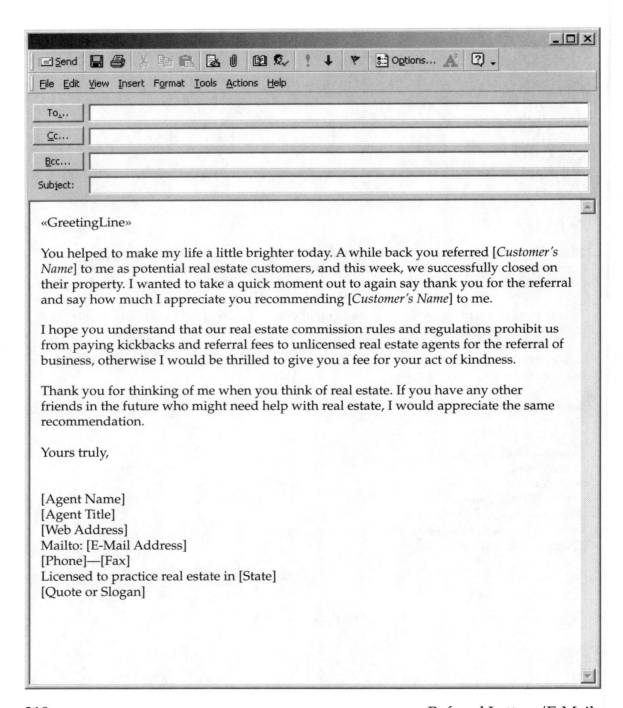

«GreetingLine»

You helped to make my life a little brighter today. A while back you referred [*Customer's Name*] to me as potential real estate customers, and this week, we successfully closed on their property. I wanted to take a quick moment out to again say thank you for the referral and say how much I appreciate you recommending [*Customer's Name*] to me.

I hope you understand that our real estate commission rules and regulations prohibit us from paying kickbacks and referral fees to unlicensed real estate agents for the referral of business, otherwise I would be thrilled to give you a fee for your act of kindness.

Thank you for thinking of me when you think of real estate. If you have any other friends in the future who might need help with real estate, I would appreciate the same recommendation.

Yours truly,

[Agent Name]
[Agent Title]
[Web Address]
Mailto: [E-Mail Address]
[Phone]—[Fax]
Licensed to practice real estate in [State]
[Quote or Slogan]

Asking for Testimony: #1

[Date]

«AddressBlock»

«GreetingLine»

Well, we've done it! The transaction's closed and hopefully your life will be back to normal shortly. I realize that moving to a new property can be a huge undertaking and can consist of a lot of stress and physical wear and tear. I hope that things have settled down now and that you are enjoying your new life and your new home.

One small request I had was a possible testimonial letter for my presentation, for my listing, and for my buyers and sellers presentation folder as well as for inclusion on my personal Web site. If I could get you to jot a few sentences about my service and our completed transaction that I could use as testimony, it would be greatly appreciated. I've enclosed a self-addressed stamped envelope for you to return this to me, or you may e-mail me a response at [*Agent's E-Mail*].

Again, thank you for your business and thank you in advance should you decide to provide a testimonial that I can use to help grow my business. I appreciate your friendship and support and look forward to helping you in the near future.

Yours truly

[Agent Name]
[Agent Title]

Asking for Testimony: #2

Dear client

Now that our transaction is complete and hopefully your life is back to normal, I was hoping if I could ask you a quick favor. As you know, my real estate business is based solely on a commission income. Therefore, unlike most workers who are compensated through a weekly or hourly salary, I only get paid if I have a successful closed transaction. Oftentimes, I'm negotiating business with people who know little about me or my company, therefore, having some testimonials from satisfied clients can have a big impact on whether I get to do business with these customers or not.

I was hoping you could provide me with a short testimonial about my service from our recent real estate transaction. Your recommendation to me as a real estate professional for those looking for a real estate agent in the near future would be a big asset to me. Your testimony does not need to be lengthy; a few sentences or one or two short paragraphs about how pleased you were with me are sufficient.

As always, thank you for your business, your friendship, and support, and thank you in advance, should you decide to include a short testimonial that I could use in procuring future business. I've included a form that has a permission disclaimer for you to use when sending the testimonial back to me in the self-addressed stamped envelope.

Thanks again, and I do appreciate your business and hope I can service you again in the near future.

Authorization Form for Testimony

We hereby authorize AGENT to use our testimony in any/all advertising marketing materials, Internet Web site, postcards, and other advertising or marketing media as AGENT deems appropriate. We also acknowledge and understand that any time we would like to have our testimony removed or pulled from said marketing endeavors that a written notice to the AGENT or the AGENT's broker would be sufficient to conclude.

_____   _____

Authorized Signature   Date

_____   _____

Authorized Signature   Date

Letters from Broker

Thank You Letter for Agent Joining the Company #1

[Date]

«AddressBlock»

«GreetingLine»

I wanted to take this opportunity to thank you for making the decision to join [Company Name]. I believe you'll find joining our company a wise and profitable decision. Not only will you find the tools and services we offer to be a plus, you'll also find the work ethic and the knowledge of our agents an additional aid in prospering your real estate career.

Please know that my phone line is always open and available should you have any questions or concerns during your career at [Company Name].

Again, welcome to our company! I know you've made a wise choice, and I look forward to a long and successful relationship with you at our organization.

Yours truly,

[Agent Name]
[Agent Title]

Thank You Letter for Agent Joining the Company #2

[Date]

«AddressBlock»

«GreetingLine»

Just a note to say "Welcome to [*Company Name*]"!

It is an honor and a privilege to have you affiliate with our organization. We pride ourselves on recruiting and hiring only the best real estate professionals in our market area, one way to uphold a premier positive image in our real estate community. I know that you will help us maintain and uphold that professional persona that [*Company Name*] strives to achieve. I am certain that you will find our tools and services an added benefit with [*Company Name*].

Again, it's an honor and a privilege to have you on board as part of our team. Please feel free to call me anytime you have questions or concerns in the near future.

I look forward to a long, prosperous, and successful relationship regarding your real estate career at [*Company Name*].

Yours truly,

[Agent Name]
[Agent Title]

Letter for Agent Who Left Company

[Date]

«AddressBlock»

«GreetingLine»

It's a great sadness and disappointment that you have left [*Company Name*]. Of course, our goal and desire is that we would never lose real estate agents under any circumstance, unfortunately, that situation could only be prevalent in a perfect world. Nevertheless, we valued your friendship and your participation as a team member with [*Company Name*].

Please remember us in the future if you decide to make another career move, you know our door is always open for you and we would love to have you back at [*Company Name*] in the future.

Yours truly,

[Agent Name]
[Agent Title]

Broker Recruitment Letters

[Date]

«AddressBlock»

«GreetingLine»

Are You Happy with Your Real Estate Career?

Although my nature and strategy is not to recruit real estate professionals from another organization, I am reminded from time to time that some agents are unhappy in their current situation and are looking for new opportunities.

If you're presently dissatisfied with where your real estate career is going and would like to hear about some of the tools and services we provide our agents, please contact me at [*Broker Phone Number*] or email me at [*Agent E-Mail*]. Please understand all inquiries and information are kept completely confidential.

I appreciate your time, and I look forward to hearing from you soon.

Yours truly,

[Agent Name]
[Agent Title]

Second Letter

[Date]

«AddressBlock»

«GreetingLine»

Lacking Tools and Services?

If you're lacking the tools and services to take your real estate career to the next level, then perhaps I can help. Hello, my name is [*Broker Name*], and I would love to visit with you regarding your real estate career at [*Company Name*]. We pride ourselves on providing the most current and necessary tools and products available to further real estate careers.

If you would like to discover the difference in what top agents are doing at [*Company Name*] and how we can help take your real estate career to the next level, please contact me at [*Broker Phone Number*] or [*Broker E-Mail*]. Please know that all inquiries and information are kept in strict confidence.

I appreciate your time, and I really would love to help you move your real estate career to the next dimension.

Yours truly,

[Agent Name]
[Agent Title]

Another Recruitment Letter

[Date]

«AddressBlock»

«GreetingLine»

It's All about Teamwork

At [*Company Name*] we pride ourselves on teamwork. To us, it's important for each and every member of our office to work together as a team. Our philosophy and commitment to this strategy has allowed us to achieve the success and company standing that we currently have in our local Multiple Listing Service. The downside to all of this is that many agents feel or believe that we are not in the market for hiring and recruiting new agents. The exact opposite is true. [*Company Name*] is always striving and looking for opportunities to add professionals like you to our real estate team.

If you have an interest or would like an opportunity to join one of the most successful teams in the area, please contact me at [*Broker Phone Number*] or [*Broker E-Mail*]. I would love to visit with you and show you how you can become a part of our team. Please understand and know that all inquiries will be kept under strict confidence.

I appreciate your time, and I look forward to hearing from you soon.

Yours truly,

[Agent Name]
[Agent Title]

Help Agent Jump-Start Their Career

[Date]

«AddressBlock»

«GreetingLine»

I'm sure you've heard the statistic that more buyers begin their search online than through any other source. Having an effective Web site and the most current and advanced technology tools is an important role for every real estate company. At [*Company Name*] we are proud to offer state of the art technology tools for our real estate professionals to aid in their business development.

You can visit [*Company Web Site Address*] and see for yourself some of the advanced features our internet portal provides consumers as well as our real estate team members.

If you believe this is an area that can help jump-start your real estate career, increase your productivity and take you to a new level in your real estate profession, please feel free to contact me today. You may reach me at [*Broker Phone Number*].

We have a limited opportunity for a select group of agents to join our [*Office Location*] and we have chosen you as a person we'd like to work with.

Again, call me at your earliest convenience if this is an opportunity that you may be interested in. Please understand that your inquiry is kept strictly confidential.

Yours truly,

[Agent Name]
[Agent Title]

New Recruitment Letter

[Date]

«AddressBlock»

«GreetingLine»

You've Been Chosen!

That's right, [*Letter Name*] you've been chosen from a select group of real estate professionals as someone who would work well with our organization. If you've been contemplating a career move and would like to see your real estate career grow even bigger, then we should talk. All interviews are kept in strict confidence and there will be no high-pressure tactics for you to join our company.

I would love the opportunity to just discuss your needs and desires as a real estate professional and how [*Company Name*] can help you.

You may reach me at [*Broker Phone Number*] or [*Broker E-Mail*]. I appreciate your time, and I look forward to hearing from you soon.

Yours truly,

[Agent Name]
[Agent Title]

Another Recruitment Letter

[Date]

«AddressBlock»

«GreetingLine»

A Change of Scenery Does Everyone Some Good

Let's face it, from time to time we can all become stale, discouraged, or in a rut. Oftentimes there's no one to blame, it's just that adding a new look, a new environment, a new brand can oftentimes bring about a new freshness.

If your real estate career has gotten to a point that you feel the need for change, and a fresh new start, consider [*Company Name*] as a place to get that recharge. We have a limited number of openings for professionals like you who we feel would be a good fit for our team.

For a confidential interview and discussion about how [*Company Name*] can provide that fresh new start you're looking for, please contact me at [*Broker Phone Number*], [*Broker E-Mail*].

Thanks for your time and remember there's no harm or damage done in a friendly conversation.

Hope to hear from you soon.

Yours truly,

[Agent Name]
[Agent Title]

Recruitment Letter

[Date]

«AddressBlock»

«GreetingLine»

I'm Impressed

In looking through our recent multiple listing statistics, I have been impressed by the number of transactions and activity you've produced. Wow! You really are on target for a great year. Probably switching real estate firms is the last thing on your mind at this point in your life; however, one never knows the happiness or satisfaction that an individual may have in their present situation.

If, and I stress the word if, you are thinking about a company change please know that I would be more than happy to discuss with you some of the great tools and services our organization has to offer. I believe that with what you're presently producing and what our company has to provide you, your numbers could grow even more.

If you would like to schedule an appointment and share with me your future goals and desires in your real estate career, I would love to listen and see if perhaps our company could be that match for you.

Again, thanks for your time, keep up the good work, and please keep the enclosed business card on file and call me when you're ready for a company change.

Yours truly,

[Agent Name]
[Agent Title]

Recruiting New Agent
Doing Well

[Date]

«AddressBlock»

«GreetingLine»

I realize that you're new to the business, but I must tell you, your numbers so far are impressive! Now that you've had a chance to settle in and experience the other agents you're working with in your office, and the company surroundings, it might be a good time to see what else is available for you as a real estate office. If you're unhappy or discouraged, you might consider [*Company Name*] as a possible company to work for in the future. At [*Company Name*] we provide a wide variety of tools and services for our agents, but most importantly a good work environment where all of our agents work as a team and support and encourage each other. If this is an environment that you think could help grow your real estate business even bigger, please feel free to give me a call.

Again, thanks for your time, keep up the good work, and please keep the enclosed business card on file and call me when you're ready for a company change.

Yours truly,

[Agent Name]
[Agent Title]

Congratulations on Award or Achievement

[Date]

«AddressBlock»

«GreetingLine»

Congratulations on your recent [*Award or Recognition*]. Wow! What a great honor and a privilege to hear about this achievement. It's always great to hear good news and accomplishments about my fellow colleagues, and I wanted to just take a quick opportunity to say *congratulations*.

Yours truly,

[Agent Name]
[Agent Title]

Selling One of Our Listings

[Date]

«AddressBlock»

«GreetingLine»

Congratulations on your successful closing at [*Property Address*]! I've heard nothing but positive and great things about you, your professionalism, and the work that you provided on this recent transaction.

Again, congratulations and thanks for selling one of our properties!

Yours truly,

[Agent Name]
[Agent Title]

Congratulations Anniversary Date with Company

[Date]

«AddressBlock»

«GreetingLine»

Congratulations on your [*Number of Years With Company*] year with [*Company*]. Wow! What an honor and privilege to have you as a part of our team.

I wanted to just take a quick opportunity to say *congratulations* on your anniversary with [*Company Name*], and I look forward to having you with us for many more years to come.

Yours truly,

[Agent Name]
[Agent Title]

Considered a Career in Real Estate

[Date]

«AddressBlock»

«GreetingLine»

Have you ever considered a career in real estate? Despite what news reports may say about the economy, now is a great time to begin a career in real estate. With the mass exodus of many real estate agents over the last few months, beginning a career in real estate at this time is actually a smart idea.

We have excellent training and support for new real estate agents, and we feel you would make a great addition to our team. If you would like to know more about why now is a good time to begin a career in real estate, please call or e-mail me at [Broker Phone Number] or [Broker E-Mail].

Thank you for your time, and I hope to hear from you soon.

Yours truly,

[Agent Name]
[Agent Title]

Consider a Career in Real Estate

[Date]

«AddressBlock»

«GreetingLine»

Have you ever considered a career in real estate? I have a FREE "Virtual Career in Real Estate" CD-ROM that I would love to provide you. This interactive CD-ROM will explain the process of getting a real estate license as well as advise you on the various opportunities and benefits of becoming a real estate professional.

To receive your free interactive CD-ROM about a career in real estate, please contact me at [*Broker Phone Number*]. The CD-ROM is FREE, and there is no obligation to work for us.

I appreciate your time, and I hope to hear from you soon.

Yours truly,

[Agent Name]
[Agent Title]

For New or Existing Agents

[Date]

«AddressBlock»

«GreetingLine»

Working at [*Company Name*] is not like working at any real estate company. We have provided an informative and interactive Web site on why a career at [*Company Name*] is a good choice for you. You can visit our website by going to [*Web Address for Career*]. You will find many excellent resources at this Web site, which you can download for *FREE*, as well as learn a lot about [*Company Name*] and why we should be your next company destination.

Thank you for your time, and I look forward to hearing your comments about our new company career Web site.

Yours truly,

[Agent Name]
[Agent Title]

Faxes and E-Mails for Scanned Documents

Response to Inspection to Another Agent

[Date]

«AddressBlock»

«GreetingLine»

As per the terms of the sales contract, the following [*Fax/Scan*] includes my client's response to the inspection at [*Property Address*].

Please let me know your client's decision on our response to the inspection.

As always, thank you for your prompt and professional attention, and I hope we can work things out on this transaction.

Yours truly,

[Agent Name]
[Agent Title]

Agent Requesting Documents on Property

[Date]

«AddressBlock»

«GreetingLine»

The following [*Facsimile/Scan*] contains the documents you requested for the transaction at [*Property Address*]. If you have any questions or are missing any other forms, please do not hesitate to give me a call.

I appreciate your interest in this property [*Agent's Name*], and I hope your clients have an interest in pursuing this home further. Thanks again!

Yours truly,

[Agent Name]
[Agent Title]

Information for Appraiser

[Date]

«AddressBlock»

«GreetingLine»

The following [*Facsimile/Scan*] contains the documents you requested for the property you're appraising at [*Property Address*]. Please let me know if there is anything else that you need to complete this appraisal. For your information, I have included some important dates we must meet to remain in compliance with this transaction.

Date for closing _____

Date appraisal needed by _____

Contact name and phone number for this file _____

As always, thank you for your prompt and professional attention.

Yours truly,

[Agent Name]
[Agent Title]

Information for Inspector

[Date]

«AddressBlock»

«GreetingLine»

The following [*Facsimile/Scan*] contains the documents you requested for the property you're inspecting at [*Property Address*]. Please let me know if there is anything else that you need to complete this inspection. It is important that we meet the scheduled inspection date listed below to remain in compliance with this transaction.

Date inspection needed by _____

Contact name and phone number for this file _____

As always, thank you for your prompt and professional attention.

Yours truly,

[Agent Name]
[Agent Title]

Information for Occupancy

[Date]

«AddressBlock»

«GreetingLine»

The following [*Facsimile/Scan*] is a request to have the property at [*Property Address*] inspected for occupancy. Please let me know if there is anything else that you need to complete this request. It is important that we have a list of all required city occupancy requirements before the date listed below to remain in compliance with this transaction.

Date occupancy inspection needed by _____

Contact name and phone number for this file _____

As always, thank you for your prompt and professional attention.

Yours truly,

[Agent Name]
[Agent Title]

Order Request for Escrow on Property

[Date]

«AddressBlock»

«GreetingLine»

The following [*Facsimile/Scan*] contains the documents for a new escrow order I wish to place on [*Property Address*]. Please let me know if there is anything else that you need to prepare for this closing.

Date of scheduled closing _____

Date papers needed for review _____

Contact name and phone numbers _____

Listing Agency _____

[Phone and E-Mail]

Listing Agent _____

[Phone and E-Mail]

Selling Agency _____

[Phone and E-Mail]

Selling Agent _____

[Phone and E-Mail]

As always, thank you for your prompt and professional attention.

Yours truly,

[Agent Name]
[Agent Title]

Submission of Offer to Purchase

[Date]

«AddressBlock»

«GreetingLine»

The following [*Facsimile/Scan*] contains the documents for the sale of your property that we discussed over the telephone. Please sign each page where indicated and return to me at the above [*Fax Number or E-Mail*]. If you have any questions, please do not hesitate to give me a call.

As always, thank you for providing me the opportunity to serve you with your real estate needs.

Yours truly,

[Agent Name]
[Agent Title]

Cover Letter for
Counter-Offer

[Date]

«AddressBlock»

«GreetingLine»

The following [*Facsimile/Scan*] contains the documents for the counteroffer for the property at [*Property Address*]. Please sign and/or initial each page where indicated and return to me at [*Fax Number or E-Mail Address*]. If you have any questions, please do not hesitate to give me a call.

As always, thank you for providing me the opportunity to serve you with your real estate needs.

Yours truly,

[Agent Name]
[Agent Title]

Referral Documents

[Date]

«AddressBlock»

«GreetingLine»

The following [*Facsimile/Scan*] contains the signed document(s) you requested for the referral agreement you plan to send to me.

I appreciate your thinking of me on this transaction, and I promise to give your client prompt, professional attention. I will keep you updated on my progress, and please do not hesitate to call me if you have any questions.

Yours truly,

[Agent Name]
[Agent Title]

Requesting Documents after Closing

[Date]

«AddressBlock»

«GreetingLine»

Could you please fax or e-mail me a completed set of copies for the transaction currently under contract at [*Property Address*]? I would like to make sure I am not missing any forms from my file. If you have any questions, please do not hesitate to give me a call. I appreciate your taking time out to do this for me.

I am pleased to be working with you, [*Agent's Name*], on this transaction, and I look forward to a smooth closing for all parties. Thanks again!

Yours truly,

[Agent Name]
[Agent Title]

Conclusion

In closing, thank you for your purchase of *"5 Minutes to More Great Real Estate Letters,"* and I wish you the best of luck with your real estate career. I hope you concur with me that daily correspondence and professional communication with your clients and customers is a major part of your success as a real estate professional. With today's technology, social media, text messaging, and other forms of informal communication tools, people can easily forget the importance of a personal touch. Remember, most people appreciate and value personal notes and letters from friends and business acquaintances, and utilizing this method of reaching out to your friends, families, and sphere of influence is essential.

I hope you will find the letters useful and an integral part of your daily business lives. Best of luck, and please let me know if I can help you.

John D. Mayfield